Programming in UNIX and Compiler Design

Programming in UNIX and Compiler Design

Dr. K. V. N Sunitha
Professor and Head Department of CSE

N. Kalyani
Associate Professor
Department of CSE

G. Narayanamma Institute of Technology and Science
Shaikpet, Hyderabad.

BSP BS Publications
A unit of BSP Books Pvt., Ltd.
4-4-309/316, Giriraj Lane,
Sultan Bazar, Hyderabad - 500 095

First Reprint 2022

Published by :

BSP BS Publications
A unit of BSP Books Pvt., Ltd.
4-4-309/316, Giriraj Lane, Sultan Bazar,
Hyderabad - 500 095
Phone : 040 - 23445688
e-mail : info@bspbooks.net
www.bspbooks.net

Printed at

Repro India Limited.

Price : Rs. 350.00

ISBN : 978-81-7800-164-7 (Paperback)

Dedicated to

our parents

Preface

There is a vast difference between knowledge and expertise. Knowledge lets you deduce the right thing to do; expertise makes the right thing a reflex, hardly requiring conscious thought at all.

This book has a lot of knowledge, but it is mainly about expertise. It is going to try to teach you the things about Unix development and designing a compiler. It is therefore less about technical and more about programming exercises than most of Unix / compiler books.

This book has great practical importance, because most of the books written for unix or compiler mainly focus on the theory but less importance is given for the practical work. Students at undergraduate level have these as their core subjects including theory and practice. This book is aimed at providing a comfortable way to attempt the problems through detailed algorithm and also with the implementation. We hope that readers of this book will learn something of what Unix has to teach about good design and how to design a simple compiler.

This book is divided into two parts: Unix programming and Compiler design. The first part focuses on Advanced Unix programming. Gives the details about how to programm in shell environment with good examples followed by the programming examples and exercises. At the end of first part exercise questions are included for the practice and with viva questions for the easy preparation for student.

Second part includes the Compiler Design. Gives brief introduction of the phases followed by the algorithm and program implementation in C. It has good explanation in details about Compiler writing tools like LEX, YACC. Each chapter includes the exercises and viva questions for student practice.

First of all, we would like to thank our parents, husbands and children for their support and co-operation. We also express our sincerely thanks to the management, Principal and collegues of G. Narayanamma Institute of Science and Technology. Finally, we would like to thank M/S BS Publications, particularly Mr. K.S. Raju for encouraging and timely bringing the book.

-Authors

Who should Read this Book

You should read this book, if you are a beginner for Unix programming and compiler designing as a student who finds it hard to follow the books which explain only theory part leaving the implementation.

You should read this book if you are a C programmer with experience on other operating systems and you are about to start a Unix-based project.

You should read this book, if you are a Unix user with novice-level up to middle-level skills in the operating system, but little development experience, and want to learn how to design software effectively under Unix or design a mini compiler for a simple language.

You should read this book if you are looking for details of shell coding or C coding for handling process or inter process communication, handling files and signals or want to design a mini compiler step by step.

How to use this Book

This book is both theory and practical. Some parts are aphoristic and general, others will examine specific case studies in Unix development and compiler design. We will precede or follow general principles and aphorisms with examples that illustrate them: examples drawn not from toy demonstration programs but rather from real working code that is in use.

We have deliberately avoided filling the book with lots of code or specification-file examples, even though in many places this might have made it easier to write (and in some places perhaps hard to follow!). Most books about programming give too many high-level details and examples, but fail at giving the reader a low-level feel for what is really going on. In this book, we prefer to move in the direction to make student comfortable. Absorbing the examples will help solidify the principles you learn into semi-instinctive working knowledge.

To make this book more accessible to less technical readers, we invited some non-programmers to read it and identify terms that seemed both obscure and necessary to the flow of exposition.

Contents

Part - I

Advanced UNIX Programming

Introduction to Unix

History of Unix and Causes for its Popularity

UNIX was originally developed at Bell Laboratories as a private research project by a small group of people starting in 1969. This group had experience with a number of different operating systems research efforts in the 1970's. The goals of the group were to design an operating system to satisfy the following objectives:

- Simple and elegant
- Written in a high level language rather than assembly language
- Allow re-use of code

Typical vendor operating systems of the time were extremely large and all written in assembly language. UNIX had a relatively small amount of code written in assembly language (this is called the kernel) and the remaining code for the operating system was written in a high level language called C.

The group worked primarily in the high level language in developing the operating system. As this development continued, small changes were necessary in the kernel and the language to allow the operating system to be completed. Through this evolution the kernel and associated software were extended until a complete operating system was written on top of the kernel in the language C.

Unix Application Programming Interface

Many proprietary operating systems have a simplified view of application behavior. The typical application reads some data from disk, tape or a terminal and does some processing. Output is produced onto disk, tape, terminal, or printer. The operating systems generally provide easy to use well-implemented facilities to support these types of facilities.

As applications become more sophisticated they need new features such as network access, multi-tasking, and interprocess communications. In traditional operating systems, these features are often hard to use, not well documented, and only callable from assembly language. When a program makes use of these features, the program may be much more complex and much more difficult to maintain.

In UNIX because the C language was written to be used to implement an operating system rather than a traditional "input-processing-output" application, use of these sophisticated features is quite easily done from the C language without writing any assembly language.

In addition, the documentation for these sophisticated features is in the same format and location as the documentation for the normal application calls.

When UNIX was distributed, users could write applications in C and easily make use of all of the operating system facilities. This allowed application developers to quickly develop much more sophisticated applications using these facilities.

The pattern of development in UNIX when adding new features such as networking is to provide an application program interface from the C language to access the new features.

In general UNIX system developers and application developers program in the same language using the same application programming interface. In typical proprietary operating systems, the operating systems programmers are programming in assembly language and have access to a many capabilities which are not available to the application developer.

Unix Networking

In 1984, the University of California at Berkeley released version 4.2 BSD which included a complete implementation of the TCP/IP networking protocols. Systems based on this and later BSD releases provided a multi-vendor networking capability based on Ethernet networking.

The networking support included, remote login, file transfer, electronic mail, and other important features.

As UNIX was ported onto more and more different types of computer hardware the UNIX networking allowed many different types of systems to share and mutually use data. Networks consisting of many different systems could be used as a large distributed system.

When SUN Microsystems added NFS (Network File System), this ability to share and mutually use data was significantly enhanced.

Unix Popularity

The application portability and system programming issues have caused many hardware and software vendors to choose UNIX. The effect of many vendors choosing UNIX is that there is a wide variety of UNIX systems available to users at attractive prices.

There are three primary causes for UNIX's popularity (and none is user interface):

- Only a very small amount of code in UNIX is written in assembly language. This makes it relatively easy for a computer vendor to get UNIX running on their system. UNIX is nearly the unanimous choice of operating system for computer companies started since 1985. The user benefit which results from this is that UNIX runs on a wide variety of computer systems. Many traditional vendors have made UNIX available on their systems in addition to their proprietary operating systems.
- The application program interface allows many different types of applications to be easily implemented under UNIX without writing assembly language. These applications are relatively portable across multiple vendor hardware platforms. Third party software vendors can save costs by supporting a single UNIX version of their software rather than four completely different vendor specific versions requiring four times the maintenance.
- Vendor-independent networking allows users to easily network multiple systems from many different vendors.

These features of UNIX have contributed to its rise in popularity since the mid 1980's

User Interface

So far, there has been no mention of the user interface for UNIX. UNIX is a good operating system for experienced programmers. The operating system was designed and implemented by experienced programmers so everything which the experienced programmer needs is present but not much else. A perfect example of this is the on-line documentation called "man-pages" or manual pages. The material is completely reference oriented with very little tutorial information. Experienced programmers find the man pages very useful but the beginning user often finds them overwhelming.

In the last few years, there has been extensive work to improve the user interface to UNIX. The most dramatic effort has been the addition of windowing interfaces on top of UNIX such as X-windows, Suntools, NextStep, Motif, OpenLook, etc. These windowing interfaces do not change UNIX itself but are built on top of UNIX to provide a more intuitive interface to UNIX. Each of the different user interfaces has some advantages and some disadvantages. Currently intensive development effort is being done on all of these Graphical User Interfaces (GUIs).

Vendors providing UNIX also have done a work to improve the user interface of their particular versions of UNIX for users without windowing interfaces. Even with all of these efforts, UNIX is weak in the end-user interface area.

User Portability

Even with a relatively poor user interface, UNIX has a following of non-programmer users. The primary reason for this is because UNIX runs on so many different computer systems ranging from small desktops to the largest computers in the world. Once a user has learned UNIX, the skills can be used on many different systems. This ability for a user to work on many different makes of computer systems without re-training is called "user portability".

Many users of other operating systems have converted to using UNIX because they felt that UNIX would be the "last" operating system they would have to learn.

Open Systems

There is a recent effort to define what is an "open system" in the international standards area. An open system is a system which allows application portability, system interoperability, and user portability between many different computer vendor hardware platforms.

UNIX is a good example of the advantages to the user having an "open system".

Basic Characteristics of Unix

Unix is, at its base level, a multi-user, multitasking, virtual memory operating system that runs on a wide variety of hardware platforms. This means that Unix is able to do many things at the same time, for many different users, and using more memory than it really has physically installed. From a user's perspective this is very nice, and from an operating systems point of view, it is very interesting. But Unix really is much more than just an operating system; it is a philosophy of using and programming a computer that gets its power from the relationships between programs rather than the programs themselves.

Let's look at each of the three characteristics of Unix listed above. Unix is a multi-user system. This means that inherent to Unix is the idea that there are different users of the system, and that different users may have different sorts of privileges and types of access to different parts of the system. It allows for the idea that some users may want to protect some of their data from being accessed by other users on the system. So, in being a multi-user system, the basic ideas of system security and data privacy come up. Likewise, there must be some way to identify one user from another in a multi-user system. Unix uses a system of login names to identify users and passwords to authenticate that a user is, in fact, who she claims to be.

Unix is a multitasking system. This means that Unix has the ability to handle more than one task at a time. These tasks might be several programs that any particular user wants to run, or they may be programs run by several users at once. Multitasking, combined with being a multi-user system, makes it possible for more than one person to be logged in and using a Unix system at once. This is true for any Unix system, not just large timesharing systems. Even small, desktop systems have the capability to support multiple concurrent users. Additionally, some of the tasks that the system could be doing, and probably is doing, can be system tasks related to keeping the system going and providing the services needed by the users.

Unix is a virtual memory operating system. The concept of virtual memory and memory management is a bit high level but a few key concepts are important to note. In a virtual memory system, the system behaves as if it has much more memory than is physically installed. Some portion of the disk is used to simulate extra memory. This idea makes it possible to run large programs on a smaller system. Some tradeoff exists between the amount of memory that a program uses and how fast it will run, since if it is very large, it must access the disk a lot, but it will eventually run. In a multitasking environment, tasks that are not currently running can be moved out of memory and onto disk to free up memory for tasks that more urgently need it. The overall result is better use of the system resources for all involved.

CHAPTER 1

Shell Programming

1.1 Introduction to Shell Scripting

The Shell as a Programming Language

You can type in a sequence of commands and allow the shell to execute them interactively, or you can sotre these commands in a file which you can invoke as a program.

Interactive Programs

A quick way of trying out small code fragments is to just type in the shell script on the command line. Here is a shell program to compile only files that contain the string "POSIX".

```
for file in *
do
if grep –l POSIX $file
then
more $file
fi
done
```

1.2 Creating a Script

To create a **shell script** first use a text editor to create a file containing the commands. For example, type the following commands and save them as first.sh

```
#!/bin/sh
#first.sh
# This file looks through all the files in the current directory for the string POSIX and
prints.
```

```
for file in *
do
  if grep –q POSIX $file
  then
    more $file
  fi
done
exit 0
```

Note: commands start with a #.

The line

```
#!/bin/sh
```

is special and tells the system to use the /bin/sh program to execute this program.

The command

```
exit 0
```

Causes the script program to exit and return a value of 0, which means there were not errors.

Making a Script Executable

There are two ways to execute the script. 1) invoke the shell with the name of the script file as a parameter, thus:

```
/bin/sh first.sh
```

Or 2) change the mode of the script to executable and then after execute it by just typing its name.

```
Chmod +x first.sh
first.sh
```

Actually, you may need to type:

```
./first.sh
```

to make the file execute unles the path variable has your directory in it.

Shell Syntax

The modern UNIX shell can be used to write quite large, structured programs.

Variables

Variables are generally created when you first use them. By default, all variables are considered and stored as strings. Variable names are case sensitive.

```
$ a=10
$ echo $a
Prints value 10
```

Quoting

Normally, parameters are separated by white space, such as a space. Single quot marks can be used to enclose values containing space(s).

```
$ a='this is first program'
```

Environment Variables

When a shell starts, some variables are initialized from values in the environment. Here is a sample of some of them.

Environment variables	*Description*
$PATH	A colon separated list of directories to search for commands.
$HOME	The home directory of the current user
$PS2	A command prompt, usually $
$PS2	Second command prompt, usually >
$IFS	An input field separated.
$0	Name of shell script
$#	Number of parameters passed
$$	Process ID of the shell script, often used inside a script for generating unique temporary file name.

Note: If your script is invoked with parameters, some additional variables are created. $1, $2…..

How it Works

It creates the variable substitution, displays its value, and some parameter variables.

Conditions

All programming languages have the ability to test conditions and perform different actions based on those conditions. A shell script can test the exit code of any command.

The Test, or []Command

Here is how to check for the existence of the file fred.c using the test and using the [] command

```
if test –f fred.c
then
……
fi
or
if [ –f fred.c ]
then
……
fi
```

or

```
if [ –f fred.c ]; then
……
fi
```

Here are the condition types that can be used with the test command. There are string comparisons.

Types of comparisons	*returns*
string	True if string is not empty
string = string	True if both are same
string != string	True if both are different
-n string	True if string is not NULL
-z string	True if string is empty

There are arithmetic comparison.

expr1 relation expr2

True if the relation is satisfied. Different relations are –eq , -ne, -gt, -lt, -ge, -le

The file conditions that can be used are -d (directory), -e (exists), -f (regular file), -g(set group id is set), -r (readable), -z (non zero file), -u (set user id is set), -w (writable), -x (executable).

Control Structures

The shell has a set of control structures.

if

The if statement is vary similar to other programming languages except it ends with a fi.

```
if condition
then
    statements
else
    statements
fi
```

elif

the elif is better known as "else if". It replaces the else part of an if statement with another if statement. You can try it out by using the following script.

```
#!/bin/sh
echo "Is it morning? Please answer yes or no"
read timeofday
if [ $timeofday = "yes" ]
then
    echo "Good morning"
elif [ $timeofday = "no" ]; then
    echo "Good afternoon"
else
    echo "Sorry, $timeofday not recognized. Enter yes or no"
    exit 1
fi
exit 0
```

How it Works

The above does a second test on the variable timeofday if it isn't equal to no.

A Problem with Variables

If a variable is set to null, the statement

```
if [ $timeofday = "yes" ]
```

looks like

```
if [ = "yes" ]
```

which is illegal. This problem can be fixed by using double quotes around the variable name.

```
if [ "$timeofday" = "yes" ]
```

for

The for construct is used for looping through a range of values, which can be any set of strings. The syntax is:

```
for variable in values
do
    statements
done
```

Try out the following script:

```
#!/bin/sh
for foo in bar fud 43
do
    echo $foo
done
exit 0
```

When executed, the output should be:

```
bar
fud
43
```

How it Works

The above example creates the variable foo and assigns it a different value each time around the for loop.

Example

Here is another script which uses the $(command) syntax to expand a list to chap3.txt, chap4.txt, and chap5.txt and print the files.

```
#!/bin/sh
for file in $(ls chap[345].txt); do
    lpr $file
done
```

While

While loops will loop as long as some condition exists. Of course something in the body statements of the loop should eventually change the condition and cause the loop to exit. Here is the while loop syntax.

```
while condition do
    statements
done
```

Here is a while loop that loops 20 times.

```
#!/bin/sh
foo=1
while [ "$foo" -le 20 ]
do
    echo "Here we go again"
    foo=$(($foo+1))
done
exit 0
```

How it Works

The above script uses the [ ] command to test foo for <= the value 20. The line

```
foo=$(($foo+1))
```

increments the value of foo each time the loop executes.

Until

The until statement loops until a condition becomes true. Its syntax is:

```
until condition
do
    statements
done
```

Here is a script using until.

```
#!/bin/sh
until who | grep "$1" > /dev/null
do
    sleep 60
done
# now ring the bell and announce the expected user.
echo -e \\a
echo "**** $1 has just loogged in ****"
exit 0
```

Case

The case statement allows the testing of a variable for more then one value. The case statement ends with the word esac. Its syntax is:

```
case variable in
    pattern [ | pattern] ...) statements;;
    pattern [ | pattern] ...) statements;;
    ...
esac
```

Here is a sample script using a case statement:

```
#!/bin/sh
echo "Is it morning? Please answer yes or no"
read timeofday
case "$timeofday" in
    "yes") echo "Good Morning";;
    "no" ) echo "Good Afternoon";;
    "y" ) echo "Good Morning";;
    "n" ) echo "Good Afternoon";;
    * ) echo "Soory, answer not recognized";;
esac
exit 0
```

How it Works

The value in the varaible timeofday is compared to various strings. When a match is made, the associated echo command is executed.

Here is a case where multiple strings are tested at a time, to do the same action.

```
case "$timeofday" in
    "yes" | "y" | "Yes" | "YES" ) echo "good Morning";;
    "n"* | "N"* ) <echo "Good Afternoon";;
    * ) < echo "Sorry, answer not recognize";;
esac
```

The above has several strings tested for each possible statement.

Here is a case statement that executes multiple statements for each case.

```
case "$timeofday" in
    "yes" | "y" | "Yes" | "YES" )
        echo "Good Morning"
        echo "Up bright and early this morning"
        ;;
[nN]*)
        echo "Good Afternoon"
        ;;
*)
        echo "Sorry, answer not recognize"
        echo "Please answer yes or no"
        exit 1
        ;;
esac
```

When a match is found to the variable value of timeofday, all the statements up to the ;; are executed.

Lists

To test for multiple conditions, we can use nested if or if/elif.

The AND List

Allows us to execute a series of commands. Each command is only executed if the previous commands have succeeded. An AND list joins conditions by using &&.

```
statement1 && statement2 && statement3 && ...
```

Here is a sample AND list:

```
#!/bin/sh
touch file_one
rm -f file_two
if [ -f file_one ] && echo "hello" && [ -f file_two ] && echo " there"
then
    echo "in if"
else
    echo "in else"
fi
exit 0
```

How it Works

The touch command creates an empty file_one the rm command remove a file_two. So, before we start, file_one exists and file_two doesn't. The AND list finds the file_one, and echos the word hello, but it doesn't find the file file_two. Therefore the overall if fails and the else clause is executed.

The OR List

The OR list construct allows us to execute a series of commands until one succeeds.

```
statement1 || statement2 || statement3 || ...
```

Here is a sample OR list

```
rm -f file_one
if [ -f file_one ] || echo "hello" || echo " there"
then
echo "in if"
else
echo "in else"
fi
exit 0
```

How it Works

The above script removes the file file_one, then test for and fails to find the file_one, but does successfully echo hello. It then executes the then statement echoing in if.

Statement Blocks

Multiple statements can be placed inside of { } to make a statement block.

Functions

You can define functions in the shell. The syntax is:

```
function_name () {
    statements
}
```

Here is a sample function and its execution.

```
#!/bin/sh
foo() {
    echo "Function foo is executing"
}
echo "script starting"
foo
echo "script ended"
exit 0
```

How it Works

When the above script runs, it defines the funcion foo, then script echos script starting, then it runs the functions foo which echos Function foo is executing, then it echo script ended.

Here is another sample script with a function in it. Save it as my_name

```
#!/bin/sh
yes_or_no() {
    echo "Parameters are $*"
    while true
    do
        echo -n "Enter yes or no"
        read x
        case "$x" in
            y | yes ) return 0;;
            n | no ) return 1;;
            * ) echo "Answer yes or no"
        esac
```

```
done
}
echo "Original parameters are $*"
if yes_or_no "Is your name $1"
then
        echo "Hi $1"
else
        echo "Never mind"
fi
exit 0
```

How it Works

When my_name is execute with the statement:

```
my_name Rick and Neil
```

. gives the output of:

```
Original parameters are Rick and Neil
Parameters are Is your name Rick
Enter yes or no
no
Never mind
```

1.3 Commands

You can execute normal command and built-in commands from a shell script. Built-in commands are defined and only run inside of the script.

Break

It is used to escape from an enclosing for, while or until loop before the controlling condition has been met.

The : Command

The colon command is a null command. It can be used for an alias for true.

Continue

The continue command makes the enclosing for, while, or until loop continue at the next iteration.

The . Command

The dot command executes the command in the current shell:

```
. shell_script
```

Echo

The echo command simply outputs a string to the standard output device followed by a newline character.

Eval

The eval command evaluates arguments and gives the result.

Exec

The exec command can replace the current shell with a different program. It can also modify the current file descriptors.

Exit n

The exit command causes the script to exit with exit code n. An exit code of 0 means success. Here are some other codes.

Exit code	Description
126	The file was not executable
127	A command was not found
>=128	A signal occurred

Export

The export command makes the variable named as its parameter available in subshells.

Expr

The expr command evaluates its arguments as an expression.

```
x = `expr $x + 1`
```

Here are some of its expression evaluations

```
expr1 | expr2  , expr1 & expr2  , expr1 = expr2 , expr1 > expr2  , expr1 >= expr2
expr1 < expr2 , expr1 <= expr2 , expr1 != expr2 , expr1 + expr2  , expr1 – expr2
expr1 * expr2  , expr1 / expr2 , expr1 % expr2
```

Printf

The printf command is only available in more recent shells. It works similar to the echo command. Its general form is:

```
printf "format string" parameter1 parameter2 ...
```

Here are some characters and format specifiers.

Format specifiers	*Description*
\\	Backslash character
\a	Alert
\b	Backspace character
\f	Form feed character
\n	Newline character
\r	Carriage return
\t	Tab character
\v	Vertical tab character
\ooo	The single character with octal value ooo

Conversion specifiers

d (decimal number) , c (character), s (string), % (%character)

Return

The return command causes functions to return. It can have a value parameter which it returns.

Set

The set command sets the parameter variables for the shell.

Shift

The shift command moves all the parameter variables down by one, so $2 becomes $1, $3 becomes $2, and so on.

Trap

The trap command is used for specifying the actions to take on receipt of signals. Its syntax is:

Trap Command Signal

Here are some of the signals.

Signal (signal number)	*Description*
HUP(1)	Hang up
INT(2)	Interrupt, Ctrl-d
QUIT(3)	Quit, Ctrl-d
ABRT(6)	Abort
ALRM(14)	Alarm
TERM(15)	Terminate

Unset

The unset command removes variables or functions from the environment.

Command Execution

The result of $(command) is simply the output string from the command, which is then available to the script.

Arithmetic Expansion

The $((...)) is a better alternative to the expr command, which allows simple arithmetic commands to be processed.

```
x=$(($x+1))
```

Parameter Expansion

Using { } around a variable to protect it against expansion.

```
#!/bin/sh
for i in 1 2
do
my_secret_process ${i}_tmp
done
```

How it Works

When the above program is run then the for loop is run for two times and it passes the argument 1-tmp and 2-tmp for the function my-secret-process function script based on how it is defined.

Here Documents

A here document is a special way of passing input to a command from a shell script. The document starts and ends with the same leader after <<. For example:

```
#!/bin/sh
cat <<!FUNKY!
this is a here
document
!FUNKY!
```

How it Works

It executes the here document as if it were input commands.

1.4 Debugging Scripts

When an error occurs in a script, the shell prints out the line number with an error. You can use the set command to set various shell option. Here are some of them.

Command Line Option	*Set option*	*Description*
sh -n <script>	set -o noexec set -n	Checks for syntax errors only. Does not execute commands.
sh -v <script>	set -o verbose set -v	Echoes commands before running them.
Sh -x <script>	set -o xtrace set –x	Echoes commands after processing on the command line.
	set -o nounset set -u	Gives an error message when an undefined variable is used.

1.5 Programming Examples

1. Write a shell script to generate a multiplication table.

Program: multiplication.sh

```
echo "This program displays multiplication table"
echo "Enter the number to display table"
read num
echo " Enter the range in which you want"
read r1 r2
i=$r1
while [ $i -le  $r2 ]
do
    al=`expr $num \*  $i`
    echo "$num  *  $i  =  $al"
    i=`expr $i + 1`
done
```

Input & Output

```
$ ./multiplication.sh
This program displays multiplication table
```

Enter the number to display table

12

Enter the range in which you want

```
1 5
12 * 1 = 12
12 * 2 = 24
12 * 3 = 36
12 * 4 = 48
12 * 5 = 60
```

2. Write a shell script that copies multiple files to a Directory

Program : filecopy.sh

```
echo " Enter the directory from which you want the files"
read dir1
echo " Enter the directory to which you want to copy"
read dir2
echo "Do you want to specify the file name 0 to skip"
read ans
if [ $ans == 0 ]; then
    for nam in ./$dir1/*
    do
    cp -i $nam ./$dir2
    done
else
    echo "enter the file name"
    read fname
    cp ./$dir1/$fname ./$dir2
fi
echo "copied"
```

INPUT & OUTPUT

```
prgs]$mkdir dir1
prgs]$ cd dir1/
dir1]$ touch file1 file2 file3
dir1]$ ls
file1  file2  file3
dir1]$ cd ..
```

```
prgs]$ mkdir dir2
prgs]$ ./filecopy.sh
Enter the directory from which you want the files
dir1
Enter the directory to which you want to copy
dir2
Do you want to specify the file name 0 to skip
1
enter the file name
file1
"copied"
prgs]$ ls ./dir2
file1
```

3. **Write a shell script, which counts the number of lines and words present in a given file.**

Program :count.sh

```
IFS=" "
echo "Enter file name"
read fname
lcount=0
wcount=0
ter=`tty`
exec < $fname
while read line
do
    lcount=`expr $lcount + 1`
    set $line
    wod=`echo $#`
    wcount=`expr $wcount + $wod `
done
echo " Number of lines are $lcount"
echo " Number of words are $wcount"
exec < $ter
```

INPUT OUTPUT

prgs]$ cat > file1.txt

This is compiler design and Advanced unix programming book.

prgs]$ chmod 777 count.sh

prgs]$ ./count.sh

Enter file name

file1.txt

Number of lines are 1

Number of words are 9

4. Write a shell script, which displays the list of all files in the given Directory.

Program: lscmd.sh

```
echo "enter the directory name to list the files"
read dir
IFS="/"
set $dir
for temp in  $*
do
    if [ $temp = "root" ]; then
    cd /$temp
    else
    cd $temp
    fi
    echo `pwd`
done
ls -l
```

INPUT

```
prgs]$ ./lscmd.sh
enter the directory name to list the files
dir1
home  prgs dir1
total 0
-rw-rw-r-- 1 prgs prgs 0 2008-03-27 21:23 file1
-rw-rw-r-- 1 prgs prgs 0 2008-03-27 21:23 file2
-rw-rw-r-- 1 prgs prgs 0 2008-03-27 21:23 file3
```

5. Write a shell script (small calculator) that adds, subtracts, multiplies and divides the given two integers. There are two division options: one returns the quotient and the other returns reminder. The Script requires 3 arguments: The operation to be used and two integer numbers. The options are add(-a), Subtract(-s), multiply(-m), quotient(-c) and reminder(-r).

Program: calculator.sh

```
echo "Welcome"
num=1
while [ $num -gt 0 ]
do
    echo " 1 ADD"
    echo " 2 SUBTRACT"
    echo " 3 MULTIPLY"
    echo " 4 DIVIDE"
    echo " Enter the operation"
    read opt
    echo "Enter  two numbers"
    read num1 num2
    case $opt in
    1. echo `expr $num1 + $num2`;;
    2. echo `expr $num1 – $num2`;;
    3. echo `expr $num1 \* $num2`;;
    4. echo "Enter option to display 5 quotient, 6 reminder"
       read  dop
       q=`expr $num1 / $num2`
       case $dop in
    5. echo $q;;
    6. r=`expr $num2 \* $q`
       r=`expr $num1 - $r`
        echo $r;;
    esac;;
 *) echo "Option not entred"
esac
echo "Do you want to perform operation if yes enter any positive number, otherwise negative number"
read num
done
```

INPUT & OUTPUT

```
prgs]$ ./calculator.sh
Welcome
 1 ADD
 2 SUBTRACT
 3 MULTIPLY
 4 DIVIDE
Enter the operation
1
Enter two numbers
10 20
30
Do you want to perform operation if yes enter any positive number, otherwise negative number
1
 1 ADD
 2 SUBTRACT
 3 MULTIPLY
 4 DIVIDE
 Enter the operation
4
Enter two numbers
34 6
Enter option to display 5 quotient, 6 reminder
5
4
Do you want to perform operation if yes enter any positive number, otherwise negative number
-1
```

6. Write a shell script to reverse the rows and columns of a matrix.

Program: mat.sh

```
# n X n Array.\par
declare -a alpha     # char alpha [Rows] [Columns];\par
                # Unnecessary declaration. Why?\par
```

```
rc=0
index=0
echo "enter number of Rows"
read Rows
echo "enter number of columns"
read Columns
num=`expr $Rows \* $Columns`
echo "number of elements $num  "
i1=1
while [ "$i1" -le "$num" ]
do
 row=`expr $rc / $Columns`
 column=`expr $rc % $Rows`
 let "index = $row * $Rows + $column"
 echo "enter element"
 read alpha[$index]
 let "rc = $rc + 1"
 echo
 let "i1 = $i1 + 1"
done
echo "The given matrix is"
row1=0
index1=0
echo
while [ "$row1" -lt "$Rows" ]
do
 column=0
 echo -n "       "
 while [ "$column" -lt "$Columns" ]
 do
  let "index1 = $row1 * $Rows + $column"
```

```
      echo -n "${alpha[index1]} "
      let "column= $column +  1"
     done
     let "row1 = $row1 +  1"
     echo
   done
   echo “The changed  matrix is”
   column=0
   index1=0
   echo
   while [ "$column" -lt "$Columns" ]
   do
    row1=0
    echo -n "       "
    while [ "$row1" -lt "$Rows" ]
    do
     let "index1 = $row1 * $Rows + $column"
     echo -n "${alpha[index1]} "
     let "row1= $row1 +  1"
    done
    let "column = $column +  1"
    echo
   done
```

INPUT & OUTPUT

```
prgs]$ ./mat.sh
enter number of Rows
3
enter number of columns
3
number of elements 9
enter element
12
```

```
enter element
43
enter element
67
enter element
23
enter element
33
enter element
55
enter element
87
enter element
12
enter element
5
"The given matrix is"
    12 43 67
    23 33 55
    87 12 5
"The changed matrix is"
    12 23 87
    43 33 12
    67 55 5
```

7. Use the cat command to create a file containing the following data. Call it mytable, use tabs to separate the fields.

```
1425    Ravi    15.65
4320    Ramu    26.27
6830    Sita    36.15
1450    Raju    21.86
```

8. Use the cat command to display the file, mytable.

```
$ cat mytable
1425   Ravi   15.65
4320   Ramu   26.27
6830   Sita   36.15
1450   Raju   21.86
```

9. Use the sort command to sort the file mytable according to the first field. call the sorted file my table (same name)

```
$ sort -n mytable
1425   Ravi    15.65
1450   Raju    21.86
4320   Ramu    26.27
6830   Sita    36.15
```

10. Print the file mytable

```
$lpr -P destinationprintername mytable
```

11. Use the who command and redirect the result to a file called myfile1. Use the more command to see the contents of myfile1.

```
$ who > myfile1
$ more myfile1
```

12. Use the date and who commands in sequence (in one line) such that the output of date will display on the screen and the output of who will be redirected to a file called myfile2. Use the more command to check the contents of myfile2.

```
$ who |tee myfile2 |more ; date
```

13. Pipe your/etc/passwd file to awk, and print out the home directory of each user.

```
$ cat /etc/passwd | awk '/home/'
winterschool:x:500:500:Winter School-IIITH:/home/winterschool:/bin/bash
```

14. Develop an interactive grep script that asks for a word and a file name and then tells how many lines contain that word.

create a file as follows

```
$ cat samplefile
this is a cat
this is a dog
this is a rat
that is a cat
that is a bat
that is a ball
```

Program grepscript.sh

```
echo " enter file name"
read file
while [ true ]
do
```

```
 echo "enter the word you want to count"
 read word
  if [ $word == "exit" ]; then
   exit
else
  x=`grep $word $file |wc -l `
  echo "this word occured for $x  times in the file"
fi
done
```

Output

```
[prgs]$ ./grepscript.sh
enter file name
samplefile
enter the word you want to count
this
this word occured for 3  times in the file
enter the word you want to count
is
this word occured for 6  times in the file
enter the word you want to count
cat
this word occured for 2  times in the file
enter the word you want to count
bat
this word occured for 1  times in the file
enter the word you want to count
exit
```

15. Repeat 14. using awk

create awkscript.sh file

Program

```
echo " enter file name"
read file
while [ true ]
do
echo "enter the word you want to count"
read word
if [ $word == "exit" ]; then
  exit
else
```

```
  x=`cat $file |awk /$word/ |wc -l `
  echo "this word occured for $x  times in the file"
fi
done
```

Output

```
$ ./awkscript.sh
enter file name
samplefile
enter the word you want to count
this
this word occured for 3  times in the file
enter the word you want to count
bat
this word occured for 1  times in the file
enter the word you want to count
exit
```

16. Write a shell script that takes a command–line argument and reports on whether it is directory, a file, or something else.

Program

```
#!/bin/sh
if [ $# -lt 1 ] ; then
  echo "use filetype.sh filename "
else
  if [ -f $1 ] ; then
    echo "it is a regular file"
  elif [ -d $1 ] ; then
    echo "it is a directory file"
  else
    echo "it is some other type of file"
  fi
fi
```

output

```
./filetype.sh dir1
it is a directory file
$ ./filetype.sh samplefile
it is a regular file
```

17. Write a shell script that accepts one or more file name as arguments and converts all of them to uppercase, provided they exist in the current directory.

Program

```
#!/bin/sh
if [ $# -lt 1 ] ; then
echo "use filetype.sh filelist"
else
for file in "$@"
      do
        if [ -e $file ] ; then
          tr "[a-z]" "[A-Z]" < $file >temp
          mv temp $file
        fi
      done
   fi
```

output

```
$ cat samplefile
this is a cat
this is a dog
this is a rat
that is a cat
that is a bat
that is a ball
[prgs]$ ./upper.sh samplefile
[prgs]$ cat samplefile
THIS IS A CAT
THIS IS A DOG
THIS IS A RAT
THAT IS A CAT
THAT IS A BAT
THAT IS A BALL
```

18. Write a shell script that determines the period for which a specified user is working on the system.

Program

```
IFS=":"
echo "enter user name"
read uname
while [ `who | grep $uname | wc -l ` -eq 0 ]
do
   sleep 5
```

```
done
stime=`date +%T`
set $stime
st=`expr $3 + $2 \* 60 + $1 \* 3600`
while [ `who | grep $uname | wc -l` -eq 1 ]
do
  sleep 5
done
etime=`date +%T`
set $etime
et=`expr $3 + $2 \* 60 + $1 \* 3600`
utime=`expr $et - $st`
echo "$uname used for $utime seconds"
```

19. Write a shell script that accepts a file name starting and ending line numbers as arguments and displays all the lines between the given line numbers.

Program

```
echo "enter starting line number"
read sline
echo " enter ending line number"
read eline
for file in "$@" ; do
exec < $file
i=1
while read line ; do
  if  [ $i -ge $sline ] && [  $i -le $eline ]  ; then
    echo $line
  fi
  i=`expr $i + 1`
done
done
```

output

```
$ ./displine.sh samplefile file2.txt
enter starting line number
2
enter ending line number
3
THIS IS A DOG
THIS IS A RAT
SMITH:ECE:PROFESSOR
JAMES:CSE:PROFESSOR
```

20. Write a shell script that deletes all lines containing a specified word in one or more files supplied as arguments to it.

PROGRAM

```
echo " enter word "
read word
for file in "$@" ; do
 `grep -v $word $file > $file.1 `
  cat $file
  cat $file.1
done
```

OUTPUT

```
./dellines.sh samplefile
enter word
CAT
THIS IS A CAT
THIS IS A DOG
THIS IS A RAT
THAT IS A CAT
THAT IS A BAT
THAT IS A BALL
file.1

THIS IS A DOG
THIS IS A RAT
THAT IS A BAT
THAT IS A BALL
```

21. Write a shell script that computes the gross salary of a employee according to the following rules

(i) If basic salary is < 1500 then HRA =10% of the basic and DA =90% of the basic.

(ii)If basic salary is >=1500 then HRA =Rs. 500 and DA=98% of the basic

The basic salary is entered interactively through the key board.

PROGRAM

```
IFS=";"
terminal="$tty"
exec < $1
while read line ; do
 set $line
 if [ $6 -lt 1500 ] ; then
  HRA=`echo "$6 * 0.1" | bc`
```

```
    DA=`echo "$6 * 0.90" |bc`
    grssal=`echo "$6 + $HRA + $DA" |bc`
  else
    DA=`echo "$6 * 0.98"|bc`
    grssal=`echo "$6 + $DA + 500 "|bc`
  fi
  echo "$2    $6    $grssal"
done
```

let the file be emp file as stated in the exercise

OUTPUT

```
$ ./grossal.sh emp
ALLEN     1700    3866.00
WARD      1350    2700.00
JONES     3075    6588.50
MARTIN    1350    2700.00
BLAKE     2950    6341.00
CLARK     4100    8618.00
SCOTT     4100    8618.00
KING      6300   12974.00
TURNER    1600    3668.00
ADAMS     5200   10796.00
JAMES     5050   10499.00
FORD      3100    6638.00
MILLER    6600   13568.00
```

22. Write a shell script that accepts two integers as its arguments and computes the value of first number raised to the power of the second number.

PROGRAM

```
echo "enter first number"
read num1
echo "enter second number"
read num2
i=1
res=$num1
while [ $i -lt $num2 ]
do
  res=`expr $res \* $num1`
  i=`expr $i + 1`
done
echo "$num1 raised to $num2 is $res"
```

OUTPUT

```
$ ./pow.sh
enter first number
2
enter second number
2
2 raised to 2 is 4
[prgs]$ ./pow.sh
enter first number
3
enter second number
3
3 raised to 3 is 27
```

23. Write an interactive file-handling Shell Program. Let it offer the user the choice of copying, removing, renaming, or linking files. Once the user has made a choice, have the program ask the user for the necessary information, such as the file name, new name and so on.

PROGRAM

```
echo -e "enter option\n1\tCopying\n2\tRenamming\n3\tRemoving\n4\tlinking\n5\
texit\ n"
read opt
while [ $opt -ne 5 ] ; do
 case $opt in
  1) echo "enter file name to copy"
     read sname
     echo " enter destination name"
     read des
     `cp $sname $des`
     echo "file copied"
     ;;
  2) echo "enter file name to be renamed"
     read sname
     echo " file to be renamed as "
     read des
     `mv $sname $des`
     echo " file renamed"
     ;;
  3) echo " enter file to be removed"
     read sname
     `rm $sname`
     echo "file removed"
     ;;
```

```
    4) echo " enter source file name"
       read sname
       echo " enter the new name to be linked"
       read lfile
       `ln $sname $lfile`
       echo "link created"
       ;;
    5) echo "thank you"
       exit
       ;;
  esac
echo -e "enter option
\n1\tCopying\n2\tRenamming\n3\tRemoving\n4\tlinking\n5\texit\n"
read opt
done
```

OUTPUT

```
$ ./filemod.sh
enter option
1       Copying
2       Renamming
3       Removing
4       linking
5       exit
1
enter file name to copy
samplefile
enter destination name
samplefile.2
file copied
enter option
1       Copying
2       Renamming
3       Removing
4       linking
5       exit
2
enter file name to be renamed
samplefile.1
file to be renamed as
samp.1
file renamed
enter option
```

```
1     Copying
2     Renamming
3     Removing
4     linking
5     exit
4
enter source file name
samp.1
enter the new name to be linked
file.1
link created
enter option
1     Copying
2     Renamming
3     Removing
4     linking
5     exit
3
enter file to be removed
file.1
file removed
enter option
1     Copying
2     Renamming
3     Removing
4     linking
5     exit
5
```

24. Write a shell script which receives two file names as arguments. It should check whether the two file contents are same or not. If they are same then second file should be deleted.

HINT

create two files with same contents
use comm with options -1,-2 and count number of lines
if it is 0 then both are same hence delete one file using rm command.

25. Write a shell script that displays a list of all the files in the current directory to which the user has read, write and execute permissions.

PROGRAM

```
for file in `ls *`
do
```

```
  x=0
  echo "$file has "
  if [ -r $file ] ; then
    echo " read permissions "
    x=1
  fi
  if [ -w $file ] ; then
    echo " write permissions"
    x=1
  fi
  if [ -x $file ] ; then
    echo "execute permissions "
    x=1
  fi
  if [ $x -eq 0 ] ; then
    echo  " no permissions "
  fi
done
```

OUTPUT

```
./lsfile.sh
a.out has
read permissions
write permissions
execute permissions
awkscript.sh has
read permissions
write permissions
execute permissions
...
semdemo.c has
no permissions
seminit has
no permissions
```

26. Develop an interactive script that ask for a word and a file name and then tells how many times that word occurred in the file.

PROGRAM

```
IFS=" "
echo "Enter file name"
read fname
```

```
echo "enter word to be counted"
read word
wcount=0
exec < $fname
while read line ; do
  set $line
  for wd in $*
  do
    if [ $word == $wd ] ; then
       wcount=`expr $wcount + 1`
    fi
  done
done
echo " Number of times the word $word occurs is $wcount"
```

OUTPUT

```
$ ./countwd.sh
Enter file name
samplefile
enter word to be counted
THIS
Number of times the word THIS occurs is 3
```

CHAPTER 2

Unix File Structure

In UNIX, everything is a file. Programs can use disk files, serial ports, printers and other devices in the exactly the same way as they would use a file.

Directories, too, are special sorts of files.

2.1 Directories

The entries in a directory contains file name and its 'administrative information', i.e. the file's creation/modification date and its permissions.

The permissions are stored in the **inode** table, which also contains the length of the file and where on the disc it's stored.

A directory is a file that holds the inodes and names of other files.

Files are arranged in directories, which also contain subdirectories.

2.2 Files and Devices

Even hardware devices are represented (mapped) by files in UNIX. For example, as **root**, you mount a CD-ROM drive as a file,

```
$ mount -t iso9660 /dev/hdc /mnt/cd_rom
$ cd /mnt/cd_rom
```

/dev/console - this device represents the system console.
/dev/tty - This special file is an alias (logical device) for controlling terminal (keyboard and screen, or window) of a process.
/dev/null - This is the null device. All output written to this device is discarded.

System Calls and Device Drivers

System calls are provided by UNIX to access and control files and devices.

A number of **device drivers** are part of the kernel.

The system calls to access the device drivers include:

Method	*Description*
open	Open a file or a device
read	Read from an open file or device
write	Write to a file or a device
close	Close the file or device
ioctl	Specific control on the device

2.3 Library Functions

To provide a higher level interface to device and disk files, UNIIX provides a number of standard libraries.

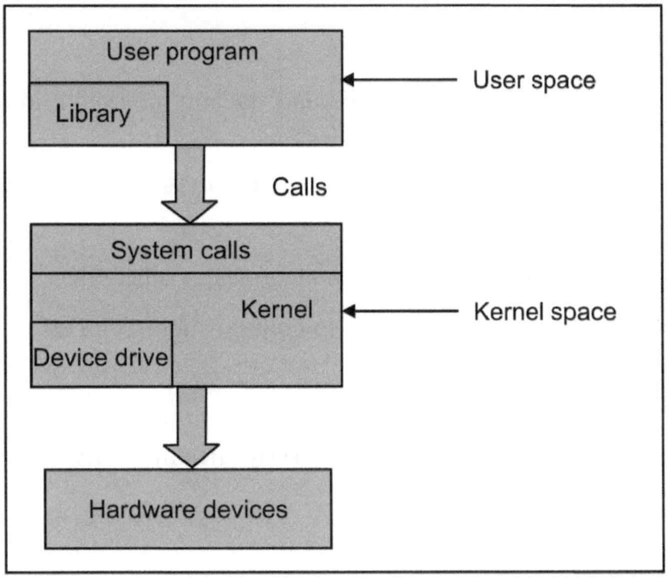

2.4 Low-level File Access

Each running program, called a **process**, has associated with it a number of file descriptors.

When a program starts, it usually has three of these descriptors already opened. These are:

Descriptor number	*Device*
0	Standard input
1	Standard output
2	Standard error

Read and Write Methods

```
#include<unistd.h>

size_t write(int fildes, const void *buf, size_t nbytes);
size_t read(int fildes, void *buf, size_t nbytes);
```

The **write** system call arranges for the first **nbytes** from **buf** to be written to the file associated with the file descriptor **fildes**.

The **read** system call reads up to **nbytes** of data from the file associated with the file decriptor **fildes** and places them in the data area **buf**.

Open

To create a new file descriptor we need to use the **open** system call. **open** establishes an access path to a file or device.

```
#include<fcntl.h>
#include<sys/types.h>
#include<sys/stat.h>

int open(const char *path, into flags);
int open(const char *path, into flags, mode_t mode);
```

The name of the file or device to be opened is passed as a parameter, **path**, and the **oflags** parameter is used to specify actions to be taken on opening the file.

The **oflags** are specified as a bitwise OR of a mandatory file access mode and other optional modes. The **open** call must specify one of the following file access modes:

File open mode	*Description*
O_RDONLY	Open for read-only
O_WRONLY	Open for write-only
O_RDWR	Open for reading and writing

The call may also include a combination (bitwise OR) of the following optional modes in the **oflags** parameter:

Oflag parameters	*Description*
O_APPEND	Place written data at the end of the file
O_TRUNC	Set the length of the file to zero, discarding existing contents.
O_CREAT	Creates the file, if necessary, with permissions given in mode.
O_EXCL	Used with O_CREAT, ensures that the caller creates the file. The open is atomic, i.e. it's performed with just one function call. This protects against two programs creating the file at the same time. If the file already exists, open will fail.

Initial Permissions

When we create a file using the **O_CREAT** flag with **open**, we must use the three parameter form. **mode**, the third parameter, is made form a bitwise OR of the flags defined in the header file **sys/stat.h**. These are:

Mode parameter	*Permissions*
S_IRUSR	Read permission, owner
S_IWUSR	Write permission, owner
S_IXUSR	Execute permission, owner
S_IRGRP	Read permission, group
S_IWGRP	Write permission, group
S_IXGRP	Execute permission, group
S_IROTH	Read permission, other
S_IWOTH	Write permission, other
S_IRXTH	Execute permission, other

Foe example

open("myfile" , O_CREAT, S_IRUSR | S_IXOTH);

Has the effect of creating a file called **myfile**, with read permission for the owner and execute permission for others, and only those permissions.

umask

The **umask** is a system variable that encodes a mask for file permissions to be used when a file is created.You can change the variable by executing the **umask** command to supply a new value.

The value is a three-digit octal value. Each digit is the results of ANDing values from 1, 2, or 4.

Digit	*Value*	*Meaning*
1	0	No user permissions are allowed.
	4	User read permission is disallowed.
	2	User write permission is disallowed.
	1	User execute permission is disallowed.
2	0	No group permissions are allowed.
	4	Group read permission is disallowed.
	2	Group write permission is disallowed.
	1	Group execute permission is disallowed.
3	0	No other permissions are allowed.
	4	Other read permission is disallowed.
	2	Other write permission is disallowed.
	1	Other execute permission is disallowed.

For example, to block 'group' write and execute, and 'other' write, the **umask** would be:

Values for each digit are ANDed together; so digit 2 will have 2 & 1, giving 3. The resulting **umask** is **032**.

Close and ioctl

```
#include<unistd.h>

int close(int fildes);
int ioctl(int fildes, int cmd, .....);
```

We use **close** to terminate the association between a file descriptor, **fildes**, and its file.

ioctl is a bit of a rag-bag of things. It provides an interface for controlling the behavior of devices, their descriptors and configuring underlying services.

ioctl performs the function indicated by **cmd** on the object referenced by the descriptor **fildes**.

lseek

```
#include<unistd.h>
#include<sys/types.h>

off_t lseek(int fildes, off_t offset, int whence);
```

The **lseek** system call sets the read/write pointer of a file descriptor, **fildes**. You use it to set where in the file the next read or write will occur.

The **offset** parameter is used to specify the position and the **whence** parameter specifies how the offset is used.

whence can be one of the following:

SEEK_SET	Offset in an absolute position
SEEK_SET	Offset is relative to the current position
SEEK_SET	Offset is relative to the end of the file

fstat, stat and lstat

```
#include<unistd.h>
#include<sys/types.h>
#include<sys/stat.h>

int fstat(int fildes, struct stat *buf);
int stat(const char *path, struct stat *buf);
int fstat(const char *path, struct stat *buf);
```

The **fstat** system call returns status information about the file associated with an open file descriptor.

The members of the structure, **stat**, may vary between UNIX systems, but will include:

Stat member	*Description*
st_mode	File permissions and file type information.
st_ino	The inode associated with the file.
st_dev	The device the file resides on.
st_uid	The user identity of the file owner.
st_gid	The group identity of the file owner.
st_atime	The time of last access.
st_ctime	The time of last change to mode, owner, group or content.
st_mtime	The time of last modification to contents.
st_nlink	The number of hard links to the file.

The permission flags are the same as for the **open** system call above. File-type flags include:

S_IFBLK	Entry is a block special device.
S_IFDIR	Entry is a directory.
S_IFCHR	Entry is a character special device.
S_IFFIFO	Entry is a FIFO (named pipe).
S_IFREG	Entry is a regular file.

S_IFLNK	Entry is a symbolic link.
S_ISUID	Entry has setUID on execution.
S_ISGID	Entry has setGID on execution.

Masks to interpret the **st_mode** flags include:

S_IFMT	File type
S_IR WXU	User read/write/execute permissions.
S_IR WXG	Group read/write/execute permissions.
S_IR WXO	Other read/write/execute permissions.

There are some macros defined to help with determining file types. These include:

S_ISBLK	Test for block special devive.
S_ISDIR	Test for directory.
S_ISCHR	Test for character special device.
S_ISFIFO	Test for FIFO (named pipe).
S_ISREG	Test for regular file.
S_ISLNK	Test for symbolic link.

To test that a file doesn't represent a directory and has execute permisson set for the owner and no other permissions, we can use the test:

Sample Code

```
struct stat statbuf;
mode_t modes;

stat("filename", &statbuf);
modes = statbuf.st_mode;

if(!S_ISDIR(modes) && (modes & S_IRWXU) == S_IXUSR)
……………..
```

dup and dup2

```
#include<unistd.h>

int dup(int fildes);
int dup2(int fildes, int fildes2);
```

The **dup** system calls provide a way of duplicating a file descriptor, giving two or more, different descriptors that access the same file.

2.5 The Standard I/O Library

The standard I/O library and its header file **stdio.h**, provide a versatile interface to low-level I/O system calls.

Three file streams are automatically opened when a program is started. They are **stdin**, **stdout**, and **stderr**.

Fopen

```
#include<stdio.h>

FILE *fopen(const char *filename, const char *mode);
```

The **fopen** library function is the analog of the low level **open** system call.

fopen opens the file named by the **filename** parameter and associates a stream with it. The **mode** parameter specifies how the file is to be opened. It's one of the following strings:

"r" or "rb"	Open for reading only.
"w" or "wb"	Open for writing, truncate to zero length.
"a" or "ab"	Open for writing, append to end of file.
"r+" or "rb+" or "r+b"	Open for update (reading & writing)
"w+" or "wb+" or "w+b"	Open for update, truncate to zero length.
"a+" or "ab+" or "a+b"	Open for update, append to end of file.

If successful, **fopen** returns a non-null **FILE** * pointer.

fread, fwrite and fclose

```
#include<stdio.h>

size_t fread(void *ptr, size_t size, size_t nitems, FILE *stream);
size_t fwrite(const *ptr, size_t size, size_t nitems, FILE *stream);
int fclose(FILE *stream);
```

The **fread** library function is used to read data from a file stream. Data is read into a data buffer given by **ptr** from the stream, **stream**.

The **fwrite** library call has a similar interface to **fread**. It takes data records from the specified data buffer and writes them to the output stream.

The **fclose** library function closes the specified **stream**, causing any unwritten data to be written.

fflush, fseek, fgetc, getc, getchar

```
#include<stdio.h>

int fflush(FILE *stream);
int fseek(FILE *stream, long int offset, int whence);
int fgetc(FILE *stream);
int getc(FILE *stream);
int getchar();
```

The **fflush** library function causes all outstanding data on a file stream to be written immediately.

The **fseek** function is the file stream equivalent of the **lseek** system call. It sets the position in the stream for the next read or write on that stream.

The **fgetc** function returns the next byte, as a character, from a file stream. When it reaches the end of file, it returns **EOF**.

The **getc** function is equivalent to **fgetc**, except that you can implement it as a macro.

The **getchar** function is equivalent to **getc(stdin)** and reads the next character from the standard input.

fputc, putc, putchar

```
#include<stdio.h>

int fputc(int c,FILE *stream);
int putc(int c,FILE *stream);
int putchar();
```

The **fputc** function writes a character to an output file stream. It returns the value it has written, or **EOF** on failure.

The function **putc** is quivalent to **fputc**, but you may implement it as a macro.

The **putchar** function is equivalent to **putc(c,stdout)**, writing a single character to the standard output.

fgets, gets

```
#include<stdio.h>

int fgets(char * s, int n , FILE *stream);
int gets(char * s);
```

The **fgets** function reads a string from an input file **stream**. It writes characters to the string pointed to by **s** until a newline is encountered, **n-1** characters have been transferred or the end of file is reached.

2.6 Programming Examples

7. Write a C Program that counts the number of blanks in a text File.

(a) using standard I/O **(b) using system calls.**

Program a: stdio.c

```
#include<stdio.h>
int main()
{
 FILE *fp;
 int  count=0,r,c;
 fp=fopen("file1.txt","r" );
 while((c=fgetc(fp))!=EOF)
  {
   printf("%c",c);
   if(isspace(c)) count++;
  }
  printf("Number of spaces are %d",count);
}
```

INPUT & OUTPUT

./stdio

This is compiler design and Advanced unix programming book.

Number of spaces are 9

Program b: syscal.c

```
#include<sys/types.h>
#include<sys/stat.h>
#include<ctype.h>
#include<fcntl.h>
#include<stdio.h>
int main()
{
 int fd, count=0,r;
 char ch;
 if((fd=open("file1.txt",O_RDONLY))<0)
 {
  printf("file open error\n");
  return 0;
 }
 else
 {
  close(0);
  dup(fd);
  while((r=read(0,&ch,1))>0)
  {
   printf("%c",ch);
   if(isspace(ch)) count++;
  }
  printf("Number of spaces are %d",count);
 }
}
```

OUTPUT

```
prgs]$ ./syscal
This is compiler design and Advanced unix programming book.
Number of spaces are 9
```

8. Implement in C the following unix commands using system calls,

(a) cat (b) Is (c) mv

Program a: catprg.c

```
#include<sys/types.h>
#include<sys/stat.h>
#include<fcntl.h>
#include<stdio.h>
#include<ctype.h>
int main(int argc, char *argv[])
{
 int fd, count=0,r;
 char ch;
 if(argc!=2)
 {
  printf("specify the file name\n");
  return 0;
 }
 if((fd=open(argv[1],O_RDONLY))<0)
 {
  printf("file open error\n");
  return 0;
 }
 else
 {
  while((r=read(fd,&ch,1))>0)
   printf("%c",ch);
 }
}
```

INPUT & OUTPUT

```
prgs]$ ./catprg
specify the file name
prgs]$ ./catprg file1.txt
This is compiler design and Advanced unix programming book.
```

Program b: lsprg.c

```
#include<sys/types.h>
#include<dirent.h>
```

```
#include<stdio.h>
#include<fcntl.h>
int main(int argc, char *argv[])
{
 DIR *dp;
 struct dirent *dirp;
 if(argc!=2)
 {
  printf("specify the directory name\n");
  return 0;
 }
 if((dp=opendir(argv[1]))<0)
 {
  printf("Cannot open directory %s\n", argv[1]);
  return 0;
 }
 else
 {
  while((dirp=readdir(dp)) >0)
   printf("%s\n",dirp->d_name);
 }
 closedir(dp);
}
```

INPUT & OUTPUT

```
prgs]$ ./lsprg
specify the directory name
prgs]$ ./lsprg dir1
.
file3
file2
..
file1
```

Program c

```
#include<sys/types.h>
#include<sys/stat.h>
#include<fcntl.h>
```

```
#include<ctype.h>
int main(int argc, char *argv[])
{
 int fd1,fd2, count=0,r;
 char ch;
 if(argc!=3)
 {
  printf("specify the required file  names\n");
  return 0;
 }
 if((fd1=open(argv[1],O_RDONLY))<0)
 {
  printf("file open error\n");
  return 0;
 }
 else
 {
  if((fd2=open(argv[2],O_WRONLY,O_CREAT))<0)
  {
   printf("cannot create the specified file\n");
   return 0;
  }
  else
  {
   while((r=read(fd1,&ch,1))>0)
     write(fd2,&ch,1);
 }
 }
 close(fd1);
 close(fd2);
}
```

INPUT

./a.out file1.txt file2.txt

cat file2.txt

This is AUP manual for B.Tech III year.

9. Write a program that takes one or more file/directory names as command line input and reports the following information on the file:

(a) File type. **(b) Number of links.**

(c) Time of last access. **(d) Read, Write and Execute permissions.**

Program: report.c

```
#include<sys/types.h>
#include<sys/stat.h>
#include<unistd.h>
#include<time.h>
int main(int argc, char *argv[])
{
 int i;
 struct stat buf;
 char *ptr;
 for(i=1;i<argc;i++)
 {
  printf("Type of %s : ", argv[i]);
  if(lstat(argv[i], &buf)<0)
  {
   printf("lstat error\n");
   continue;
  }
  if(S_ISREG(buf.st_mode)) ptr="regular";
  else if(S_ISDIR(buf.st_mode)) ptr="directory";
  else if(S_ISCHR(buf.st_mode)) ptr="character special";
  else if(S_ISBLK(buf.st_mode)) ptr="blocl special";
  else if(S_ISFIFO(buf.st_mode)) ptr="fifo ";
  else if(S_ISLNK(buf.st_mode)) ptr="symbolic link";
  else if(S_ISSOCK(buf.st_mode)) ptr="socket";
  else ptr="unknown mode";
  printf(" is %s\n",ptr);
  printf("Number of links to this file are %d\n",buf.st_nlink);
  printf("Time of last access %E",buf.st_atime);
  printf("The permissions are\n");
```

```
  if(access(argv[i],R_OK)==0) printf("Read permission\t");
  if(access(argv[i],W_OK)==0)printf("Write permission\t");
  if(access(argv[i],X_OK)==0)printf("execute permission");
  printf("\n\n");
 }
}
```

INPUT & OUTPUT

```
./a.out  file1.txt

Type of file1.txt is regular,
Number of links to this file are 1
The permissions are Read permission Write permission Execute permission

./a.out  dir1
Type of dir1  is directory
Number of links to this file are 3
The permissions are Read permission Write permission Execute permission
```

CHAPTER 3

Processes

Processes form fundamental part of the UNIX operating environment, controlling almost all activities performed by a UNIX computer system.

Here are some of the things you need to understand.

3.1 What is a Process?

The X/Open Specification defines a process as an address space and single thread of control that executes within that address space and its required system resources.

A process is, essentially, a running program.

3.2 Process Structure

Here is how a couple of processes might be arranged within the operationg system.

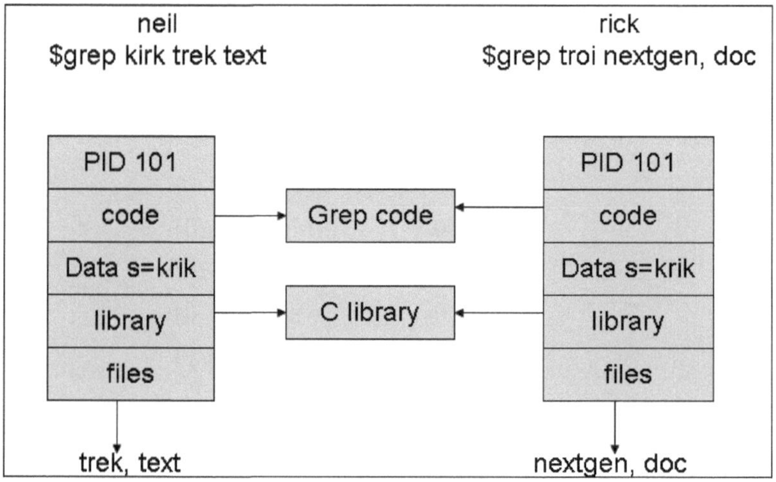

Each process is allocated a unique number, a **process identifier**, or PID.

The program code that will be executed by the **grep** command is stored in a disk file.

The system libraries can also be shared.

A process has its own stack space.

3.3 The Process Table

The UNIX **process table** may be thought of as a data structure describing all of the processes that are currently loaded.

Viewing Processes

We can see what processes are running by using the **ps** command.

Here is some sample output:

prgs]$ ps

PID	TTY	TIME	CMD
2922	pts/0	00:00:00	bash
2960	pts/0	00:00:00	ps

The **PID** column gives the PIDs, the **TTY** column shows which terminal started the process, the **STAT** column shows the current status, **TIME** gives the CPU time used so far and the **COMMAND** column shows the command used to start the process.

3.4 System Processes

Let's look at some other processes running on this Linux system. The output has been abbreviated for clarity:

prgs]$ ps -ax

PID	TTY	STAT	TIME	COMMAND
1	?	Ss	0:00	init [5]
2	?	S<	0:00	[kthreadd]
3	?	S<	0:00	[migration/0]
4	?	S<	0:00	[ksoftirqd/0]
5	?	S<	0:00	[watchdog/0]
6	?	S<	0:00	[migration/1]
7	?	S<	0:00	[ksoftirqd/1]
8	?	S<	0:00	[watchdog/1]
2922	pts/0	Ss	0:00	bash
2965	pts/0	R+	0:00	ps -ax

3.5 Process Scheduling

One further **ps** output example is the entry for the **ps** command itself:

2965 pts/0 R+ 0:00 ps -ax

This indicates that process 2965 is in a run state (**R**) and is executing the command **ps-ax**.

We can set the process priority using **nice** and adjust it using **renice**, which reduce the priority of a process by 10. High priority jobs have negative values.

Using the **ps -l** (forlong output), we can view the priority of processes. The value we are interested in is shown in the **NI** (nice) column:

```
prgs]$ ps -l
F S UID  PID   PPID  C PRI  NI ADDR SZ  WCHAN  TTY    TIME      CMD
0 S 500  2922  2918  0 80   0 -  1210   wait   pts/0  00:00:00  bash
0 R 500  2986  2922  0 80   0 -  1120   -      pts/0  00:00:00  ps
```

3.6 Starting New Processes

We can cause a program to run from inside another program and thereby create a new process by using the **system**. library function.

```
#include<stdio.h>

int  system(const *string);
```

The **system** function runs the command passed to it as **string** and waits for it to complete.

The command is executed as if the command,

$ sh –c string

has been given to a shell.

Try It Out - system

1. We can use **system** to write a program to run **ps** for us.

```
#include<stdlib.h>
#include<stdio.h>
int main()
{
   printf("Running ps with system\n");
   system("ps –ax");
   printf("Done.\n);
   exit(0);
}
```

2. When we compile and run this program, **system.c**, we get the following:

```
prgs]$ ./a.out
Running ps with system
PID     TTY     STAT    TIME    COMMAND
1       ?       Ss      0:00    init [5]
2       ?       S<      0:00    [kthreadd]
3       ?       S<      0:00    [migration/0]
4       ?       S<      0:00    [ksoftirqd/0]
5       ?       S<      0:00    [watchdog/0]
3021    pts/0   S+      0:00    ./a.out
3022    pts/0   R+      0:00    ps -ax
Done
```

3. The **system** function uses a shell to start the desired program.

   We could put the task in the background, by changing the function call to the following:

   system("ps –ax &");

   Now, when we compile and run this version of the program, we get:

```
prgs]$ ./a.out
Running ps with system
Done
  PID     TTY     STAT    TIME    COMMAND
  1       ?       Ss      0:00    init [5]
  2       ?       S<      0:00    [kthreadd]
  3       ?       S<      0:00    [migration/0]
  4       ?       S<      0:00    [ksoftirqd/0]
  5       ?       S<      0:00    [watchdog/0]
  3021    pts/0   S+      0:00    ./a.out
  3022    pts/0   R+      0:00    ps -ax
```

How it Works

In the first example, the program calls **system** with the string **"ps -ax"**, which executes the **ps** program. Our program returns from the call to **system** when the **ps** command is finished.

In the second example, the call to **system** returns as soon as the shell command finishes. The shell returns as soon as the **ps** program is started, just as would happen if we had typed,

$ ps –ax &

at a shell prompt.

10. Write a C program that illustrates how to execute two commands concurrently with a command Pipe

3.7 Executing Two Processes Concurrently

```
#include<stdlib.h>
#include<stdio.h>
int main()s
{
   printf("Execute two commands concurrently with a command pipe \n");
   system("cut –d: -f 1,2 file2.txt| wc -l");
   printf("Done.\n);
   exit(0);
}
```

Create a file file2.txt with contents as follows

```
Jim:CSE:Reader
Smith:ECE:Professor
James:CSE:Professor
```

when the program is executed then it would display the number of lines.

OUTPUT

```
prgs]$ ./pipe
Execute two commands concurrently with a command pipe
3
Done.
```

3.8 Duplicating a Process Image

To use processes to perform more than one function at a time, we need to create an entirely separate process from within a program.

We can create a new process by calling **fork**. This system call duplicates the current process.

Combined with **exec, fork** is all we need to create new processes to do our bidding.

```
#include<sys/types.h>
#include<unistd.h>

pid_t fork(void);
```

The **fork** system call creates a new child process, identical to the calling process except that the new process has a unique process ID and has the calling process as its parent PID.

A typical code fragment using **fork** is:

```
pid_t new_pid;
new_pid =fork();
switch(new_pid)
{
   case -1: /*   Error  */
        break;
   case 0:  /* Child process */
        break;
   default: /* parent process */
    break;
}
```

How It Works

When the call to **fork** is made, this program divides into two separate processes and returns 0 to child process, pid of process is returned to parent process. If fork is failed then it returns –1

11.Write a C program that illustrates the creation of child process using fork system call

Program : createps.c

```
#include<sys/types.h>
#include<sys/stat.h>
#include<unistd.h>
int main()
{
 int pid,i,j;
 printf("this is main process");
 if((pid=fork())==0)
 {
```

```
    for(i=0;i<10;i++)
    {
     printf(" Child process prints %d\n", i);
    }
  }
  else if(pid>0)
  {
    for(j=10;j<20;j++)
     printf("parent process prints %d\n",j);
  }
  else
    printf("Could not create child process\n");
  return 0;
}
```

INPUT & OUTPUT

```
./a.out
This is main process
Child process prints 0
Child process prints 1
Child process prints 2
Child process prints 3
Child process prints 4
parent process prints 10
parent process prints 11
parent process prints 12
parent process prints 13
parent process prints 14
parent process prints 15
parent process prints 16
parent process prints 17
parent process prints 18
parent process prints 19
Child process prints 5
Child process prints 6
Child process prints 7
Child process prints 8
Child process prints 9
```

Note : This order may not be same always.

CHAPTER 4

Time and Date

4.1 Introduction

It can be useful for a program to be able to determine the time and date.

Times are handled using a defined type, a **time_t**. The variable and functions for manipulating time values are in the header file **time.h**.

```
#include<time.h>

time_t time(time_t *tloc);
double difftime(time_t time1, time_t time2);
struct tm *gmtime(const time_t timeval);
```

How it Works

The function **time** with a null pointer argument, returns the time and date as a number of seconds.

The function **difftime**, that will calculate the difference in seconds between two **time_t** values and return it as a **double**.

The function **gmtime** breaks down a low-level time value into a structure containing more usual fields:

The structure **tm** is defined to contain at least the following members:

tm member	*Description*
int tm_sec	Seconds, 0-61
int tm_min	Minutes, 0-59
int tm_hour	Hours, 0-23
int tm_mday	Day in the month, 1-31
int tm_mon	Month in the year, 0-11 (January =0)
int tm_year	Years since 1900.
int tm_wday	Day in the week, 0-6(Sunday =0)
int tm_yday	Day in the year, 0-365.
int tm_isdst	Daylight savings in effect

The range for **tm_sec** allows for the occasional leap second, or double leap second.

Try it Out - gmtime

Here's a program, **gmtime.c**, that prints out the current time and date using the **tm** structure and **gmtime**:

```
#include <time.h>
#include<stdio.h>
{
    struct tm *tm_ptr;
    time_t the_time;
    (void) time(&the_time);
    tm_ptr = gmtime(&the_time);
    printf("Raw time is %ld\n",the_time);
    printf("gmtime gives:\n");
    printf("date : %02d/%%02d/%02d\n",
        tm_ptr->tm_year, tm_ptr->tm_mon+1, tm_ptr->tm_mday);
    printf("Time : %02d:%%02d:%02d\n",
        tm_ptr->tm_hour, tm_ptr->tm_min, tm_ptr->tm_sec);
    exit(0);
}
```

When we run this program, we get a good approximation of the time and date:

```
OUTPUT
prgs]$ ./a.out
Raw time is 1206661771
gmtime gives:
date : 08/02/03

Time : 23:02:49
```

How it Works

The program calls **time** to get the low-level time value and then calls **gmtime** to convert this into a structure with useful time and date values. It then prints it out.

To see the local time, we need to use the function **localtime** function and to convert a broken-down **tm** structure into a raw **time_t** value, we can use the functiion **mktime**.

```
#include<time.h>

struct  tm *localtime(const time_t *timeval);
time_t mktime(struct tm *timeptr);
char *asctime(const struct tm *timeptr);
char *ctime(const time_t *timeval);
size_t strftime(char *s, size_t maxsize, const char *format, struct tm timeptr);
char *strtime(const char *buf, const char *format, struct tm timeptr);
```

The **asctime** function returns a string that represents the time and date given by the **tm** structure **timeptr**. The string returned has a format similar to:

Mon Nov 20 12:30:34 2007\n\0

It's always a fixed format, 26 characters long. The function **ctime** is equivalent to calling: **asctime(localtime(timeval))**

The **strftime** function gives more control to the formatting of time and date. The **strftime** program obtains the current local time by calling **time** and **localtime**. It then converts it to readable form. It then uses **strptime** to extract the raw time and date and print them.

We can use the **strptime** function to convert a string to a **tm** structure.

Try it Out - ctime

Let's see **ctime** in action, using the following code:

```
#include<time.h>
#include<stdio.h>
int main()
{
   time_t timeval;
   (void)time(&timeval);
   printf("The date is %s ", ctime(&timeval));
   exit(0);
}
```

Compile and run the surprisingly named **ctime.c** and you should see:

```
$ ctime
The date is: Mon Nov 20 12:50:27 2007
```

How it Works

The **ctime.c** program calls **time** to get the low level time value and lets **ctime** do all the hard work converting it to a readable string, which it then prints.

The **format** string is used to control the characters written to the string

The conversion specifiers include:

Conversion Specifier	*Description*
%a	Abbrivated weekday name
%A	Full weekday name
%b	Abbrivated month name
%B	Full month name
%c	Date and time
%d	Day of the month, 01-31
%H	Hour, 00-23
%I	Hour in 12 hour clock, 01-12
%j	Day of the year, 001-366
%m	Month of the year, 01-12
%M	Minutes , 00-59
%p	a.m or p.m
%s	Seconds, 00-61
%u	Day in the week, 1-7(1=M0nday)
%U	Week in the year, 01-53(Sunday is the first day of the week)
%V	Week in the year, 01-53(Monday is the first day of the week)
%w	Day in the week, 0-6(0=Sunday)
%x	Date in local format
%X	Time in local format
%y	Last two digits of the year number, 00-99
%Y	Year
%Z	Time zone name
%%	A% character

12. Write a C program that displays the real time of a day every 60 seconds.

4.2 Programming Examples

```
#include<time.h>

#include<stdio.h>

#include<unistd.h>
```

```
int main()
{
   int i;
   time-t the_time;
   for(i=1;i<=10;i++)
   {
     the_time = time((time_t *) 0);
      printf("The time is %ld \n", the_time);
      sleep(6);
   }
   exit(0);
 }
```

When we run this program, it prints the low-level time value every two seconds for 20 seconds.

OUTPUT

```
prgs]$ ./a.out
The time is 1206661974
The time is 1206661980
The time is 1206661986
The time is 1206661992
The time is 1206661998
The time is 1206662004
The time is 1206662010
```

CHAPTER 5

Semaphores

5.1 Introduction

Semaphores can be thought of as really generic advisory locking mechanisms. You can use them to control access to files, shared memory, any resource to be shared among different processes. The basic functionality of a semaphore is that you can set it, or check it, or wait until it clears then set it ("test-n-set").

With System V IPC, you don't maintain a single semaphores for each resource but can have set of resources controlled by a single semaphore making the control easy.

5.2 How do you Create the Semaphore Set?

It's done with a call to semget(), which returns the semaphore id (hereafter referred to as the *semid*):

```
#include <sys/sem.h>

int semget(key_t key, int nsems, int semflg);
```

What's the *key*?

It's a unique identifier that is used by different processes to identify this semaphore set. (This ***key*** will be generated using ftok().)

The next argument, ***nsems***, is the number of semaphores in this semaphore set. The exact number is system dependent, but it's probably between 500 and 2000. If you're needing more create another semaphore set.

Final argument, ***semflg,*** this tells semget() what the permissions should be on the new semaphore set, whether you're creating a new set or just want to connect to an existing one, and other things that you can look up. For creating a new set, you can bit-wise or the access permissions with IPC_CREAT.

Here's an example call that generates the *key* with ftok() and creates a 10 semaphore set, with 666 (rw-rw-rw-) permissions:

```
#include <sys/ipc.h>
#include <sys/sem.h>

key_t key;
int semid;

key = ftok("/home/beej/somefile", 'E');
semid = semget(key, 10, 0666 | IPC_CREAT);
```

Compile the code which has this fragment of code and run it. This creates a semaphore which can be checked by using ***ipcs*** command.

Note: After the use don't forget to remove the semaphore using ipcrm.

5.3 How to use a Semaphore?

All operations that set, get, or test-n-set a semaphore use the semop() system call.

```
#include <sys/sem.h>

int semop(int semid ,struct sembuf *sops, unsigned int nsops);
```

semid argument is the number obtained from the call to semget().

sops, is a pointer to the struct sembuf that you filled with your semaphore commands. If you want, you can make an array of struct sembufs in order to do a whole bunch of semaphore operations at the same time.

nsop indicates the number of sembufs send, default is 1 if you are sending only one semaphore.

This system call is general purpose, and its functionality is dictated by a structure that is passed to it, struct sembuf:

```
struct sembuf {
    ushort sem_num;
    short sem_op;
    short sem_flg;
};
```

sem_num is the number of the semaphore in the set that you want to manipulate. ***sem_op*** is what you want to do with that semaphore. This takes on different meanings, depending on whether sem_op is positive, negative, or zero, as shown in the Table 1.

Table 1 sem_op values and their effects.

sem_op	What happens
Positive	The value of sem_op is added to the semaphore's value. This is how a program uses a semaphore to mark a resource as allocated.
Negative	If the absolute value of sem_op is greater than the value of the semaphore, the calling process will block until the value of the semaphore reaches that of the absolute value of sem_op. Finally, the absolute value of sem_op will be subtracted from the semaphore's value. This is how a process releases a resource guarded by the semaphore.
Zero	This process will wait until the semaphore in question reaches 0.

sem_flg field allows the program to specify flags the further modify the effects of the semop() call.

One of these flags is **IPC_NOWAIT** which, as the name suggests, causes the call to semop() to return with error **EAGAIN** if it encounters a situation where it would normally block. This is good for situations where you might want to "poll" to see if you can allocate a resource.

Another very useful flag is the **SEM_UNDO** flag. This causes semop() to record, in a way, the change made to the semaphore. When the program exits, the kernel will automatically undo all changes that were marked with the SEM_UNDO flag. Of course, your program should do its best to deallocate any resources it marks using the semaphore, but sometimes this isn't possible when your program gets a SIGKILL or some other unknown crash occurs.

So, basically, what you do is load up a struct sembuf with whatever values you want, then call semop()

5.4 How to Destroy a Semaphore?

There are two ways to delete a semaphore:

using Unix command **ipcrm,** or using system call **semctl()** with the proper arguments.

```
#include <sys/sem.h>

int semctl(int semid, int semnum, int cmd, union semun arg);
```

cmd should be set to IPC_RMID, which tells semctl() to remove this semaphore set.

semun provides a way to pass either an int, a struct semid_ds, or a pointer to a ushort.

```
union semun {
   int val;               /* used for SETVAL only */
   struct semid_ds;       *buf; /* for IPC_STAT and IPC_SET */
   ushort *array;         /* used for GETALL and SETALL */
};
```

The two parameters *semnum* and *arg* have no meaning in the IPC_RMID context and can be set to anything.

Here's an example call to torch a semaphore set:

```
union semun dummy;
int semid;
.
.
semid = semget(...);
.
.
semctl(semid, 0, IPC_RMID, dummy);
```

Easy peasy.

Note

When you first create some semaphores, they're all initialized to zero. This is bad, since that means they're all marked as allocated; it takes another call (either to semop() or semctl() to mark them as free. What does this mean? Well, it means that creation of a semaphore is not *atomic* (in other words, a one-step process). If two processes are trying to create, initialize, and use a semaphore at the same time, a race condition might develop.

13. Write a C program that illustrates file locking using semaphores.

Method

The first, seminit.c, creates and initializes the semaphore.
Try using ipcs from the command line to verify that it exists.
The second, semdemo.c, performs some pretend file locking using the semaphore.
The third, semrm.c is used to destroy the semaphore.

Program

Here's seminit.c (run this first!):

```
#include <stdio.h>
#include <stdlib.h>
```

```
#include <errno.h>
#include <sys/types.h>
#include <sys/ipc.h>
#include <sys/sem.h>
 union semun {
 int val;
 struct semid_ds *buf;
 unsigned short *array;
};
int main(void)
{
    key_t key;
    int semid;
    union semun arg;
if  ((key = ftok("semdemo.c", 'J')) == -1) {
    perror("ftok");
    exit(1);
}
/* create a semaphore set with 1 semaphore: */
if  ((semid = semget(key, 1, 0666 | IPC_CREAT)) == -1) {
    perror("semget");
    exit(1);
}
/* initialize semaphore #0 to 1: */
arg.val = 1;
if  (semctl(semid, 0, SETVAL, arg) == -1) {
    perror("semctl");
    exit(1);
}
    return 0;
}
```

Here's semdemo.c:

```
#include <stdio.h>
#include <stdlib.h>
#include <errno.h>
#include <sys/types.h>
```

```
#include <sys/ipc.h>
#include <sys/sem.h>
int main(void)
{
    key_t key;
    int semid;
    struct sembuf sb = {0, -1, 0};  /* set to allocate resource */
    if  ((key = ftok("semdemo.c", 'J')) == -1) {
        perror("ftok");
        exit(1);
}
/* grab the semaphore set created by seminit.c: */
if  ((semid = semget(key, 1, 0)) == -1) {
    perror("semget");
    exit(1);
}
printf("Press return to lock: ");
getchar();
printf("Trying to lock...\n");
if  (semop(semid, &sb, 1) == -1) {
    perror("semop");
    exit(1);
}
printf("Locked.\n");
printf("Press return to unlock: ");
getchar();
sb.sem_op = 1; /* free resource */
if (semop(semid, &sb, 1) == -1) {
    perror("semop");
    exit(1);
}
printf("Unlocked\n");
return 0;
}
```

Here's semrm.c:

```
#include <stdio.h>
#include <stdlib.h>
```

```
#include <errno.h>
#include <sys/types.h>
#include <sys/ipc.h>
#include <sys/sem.h>
    union semun {
    int val;
    struct semid_ds *buf;
    unsigned short *array;
};
int main(void)
{
    key_t key;
    int semid;
    union semun arg;
if  ((key = ftok("semdemo.c", 'J')) == -1) {
    perror("ftok");
    exit(1);
}
/* grab the semaphore set created by seminit.c: */
if  ((semid = semget(key, 1, 0)) == -1) {
    perror("semget");
    exit(1);
}
/* remove it: */
If  (semctl(semid, 0, IPC_RMID, arg) == -1) {
    perror("semctl");
    exit(1);
}
return 0;
}
```

Output

```
 ipcs -s
------ Semaphore Arrays --------
key     semid    owner    perms    nsems
as]$ ./seminit
as]$ ipcs -s
```

```
------ Semaphore Arrays --------
key           semid     owner        perms    nsems
0x4d07e90d    65536     wintersch    600      8
0x4a07e57b    98305     wintersch    666      1
as]$ ./semdemo
Press return to lock:
Trying to lock...
Locked.
Press return to unlock:
Unlocked
```

Try the same command in the other window and try to get lock it is not granted

```
as]$ ./semdemo
Press return to lock:
Trying to lock...
Unlocked
as]$ ./semdemo
Press return to lock:
Trying to lock...
Locked.
Press return to unlock:
Unlocked
as]$ ipcs -s
------ Semaphore Arrays --------
key           semid    owner        perms    nsems
0x4d07e90d    65536    wintersch    600      8
0x4a07e57b    98305    wintersch    666      1
as]$ ./semrm
as]$ ipcs -s
```

14 Write a C program that implements a producer-consumer system with two processes. using semaphores)

5.5 Programming Examples

```
#include<semaphore.h>
#include<sys/sem.h>
#include<sys/types.h>
```

```
#include<sys/ipc.h>
#include<ctype.h>
#include<stdio.h>
#include<sys/stat.h>
#define NBUFF 10
#define SEM_MUTEX "mutex";
#define SEM_NEMPTY " nempty"
#define SEM_NSTORED "nstored"
    int nitems;
    struct{
    int buff[NBUFF];
    sem_t *mutex, *nempty, *nstored;
    }shared;
void *produce(void *), *consume(void *);
int main(int argc, char **argv)
{
    pthread_t tid_produce, tid_consume;
    if(argc !=2)
{
    printf("usage : prodcons1 <#items>");
    return 0;
}
nitems=atoi(argv[1]);
shared.mutex=sem_open(px_ipc_name(SEM_MUTEX),O_CREAT , FILE_MODE,1
);
shared.nempty=sem_open(px_ipc_name(SEM_NEMPTY),O_CREAT|O_EXCL,
FILE_MODE, NBUFF);
shared.nstored=sem_open(px_ipc_name(SEM_NSTORED), O_CREAT |O_EXCEL,
FILE_MODE,0);
    set_concurrency(2);
    pthread_create(&tid_produce, NULL,produce,NULL);
    pthread_join(&tid_consume,NULL,consume,NULL);
    pthread_join(tid_produce,NULL);
    pthread_join(tid_consume,NULL);
    sem_unlink(px_ipc_name(SEM_MUTEX);
    sem_unlink(px_ipc_name(SEM_NEMPTY);
```

```
    sem_unlink(px_ipc_name(SEM_NSTORED);
    return 0;
}
void *produce(void *argv)
{
    int i;
    for(i=0;i<nitems;i++)
    {
    sem_wait(shared.nempty);
    sem_wait(shared.mutex);
    shared.buff[i%NBUFF] =i;
    sem_post(shared.mutex);
    sem_post(shared.nstored);
}
return(NULL);
}
void *consume(void *argv)
{
int i;
for(i=0;i<nitems;i++)
{
    sem_wait(shared.nstored);
    sem_wait(shared.mutex);
    if(shared.buff[i%NBUFF] != i)
    printf("buff[%d] = %d\n",i,shared.buff[i%NBUFF]);
    sem_post(shared.mutex);
    sem_post(shared.nempty);
}
return (NULL);
}
```

5.6 Conclusions

Whenever you have multiple processes running through a critical section of code, you need semaphores. Semaphores are very useful in a concurrency control. They're often faster than regular file locks, you can use them on other things that aren't files, such as Shared Memory Segments.

CHAPTER 6

Shared Memory Segments

Shared memory segments is a segment of memory that is shared between processes. You can connect to the shared memory segment, and get a pointer to the memory. You can read and write to this pointer and all changes you make will be visible to everyone else connected to the segment.

6.1 How to Create a Shared Memory?

Shared memory segment is created and connected to via the shmget() call:

```
#include <sys/shm.h>
int shmget(key_t key, size_t size, int shmflg);
```

Upon successful completion, shmget() returns an identifier for the shared memory segment.

The ***key*** argument should be created using ftok().

The next argument, ***size***, is the size in bytes of the shared memory segment.

Finally, the ***shmflg*** should be set to the permissions of the segment bitwise-ORd with **IPC_CREAT** if you want to create the segment, but can be 0 otherwise. (It is not required to specify IPC_CREAT every time–it will simply connect you if the segment already exists.)

Here's an example call that creates a 1K segment with 644 permissions (rw-r--r--):

```
key_t key;
int shmid;

key = ftok("/home/beej/somefile3", 'R');
shmid = shmget(key, 1024, 0644 | IPC_CREAT);
```

How do you get a pointer to that data available in shared memory?

The answer to this is **shmat()**call:

```
#include <sys/shm.h>

void *shmat(int shmid, void *shmaddr, int shmflg);
```

shmat() returns -1 on failure.

shmid is the shared memory ID you got from the call to shmget().

shmaddr, which you can use to tell shmat() which specific address to use but you should just set it to 0 and let the OS choose the address for you.

shmflg can be set to SHM_RDONLY if you only want to read from it, 0 otherwise.

Here's a more complete example of how to get a pointer to a shared memory segment:

```
key_t key;
int shmid;
char *data;

key = ftok("/home/beej/somefile3", 'R');
shmid = shmget(key, 1024, 0644 | IPC_CREAT);
data = shmat(shmid, (void *)0, 0);
```

Note: shmat() returns a void pointer, and we're treating it, in this case, as a char pointer. You can treat it as anything you like, depending on what kind of data you have choosen while returning. Pointers to arrays of structures are just as acceptable as anything else.

```
data = shmat(shmid, (void *)0, 0);
if (data == (char *)(-1))
   perror("shmat");
```

All you have to do now is change the data it points to normal pointer-style. There are some samples in the next section.

6.2 How do you Access or Add Data in Shared Memory?

Lets say you have the data pointer from the above example. It is a char pointer, so we'll be reading and writing chars from it. Furthermore, for the sake of simplicity, lets say the 1K shared memory segment contains a null-terminated string.

It couldn't be easier. Since it's just a string in there, we can print it like this:

```
printf("shared contents: %s\n", data);
```

And we could store something in it as easily as this:

```
printf("Enter a string: ");

gets(data);
```

You can access any type of data based on the datatype it is assigned.

6.3 How do you Detach from Shared Memory?

When you're done with the shared memory segment, your program should detach itself from it using the shmdt() call or shmctl call.

```
#include <sys/shm.h>

int shmdt(void *shmaddr);
shmctl(shmid, IPC_RMID, NULL);
```

The only argument, ***shmaddr***, is the address you got from shmat(). The function returns -1 on error, 0 on success.

When you detach from the segment, it isn't destroyed. Nor is it removed when *everyone* detaches from it. You have to specifically destroy it using a call to shmctl(), The above call deletes the shared memory segment, assuming no one else is attached to it. It can also be destroyed by using **ipcrm** command

6.4 What are Concurrency Issues?

Since you have multiple processes modifying the shared memory segment, it is possible that certain errors could crop up when updates to the segment occur simultaneously. This *concurrent* access is almost always a problem when you have multiple writers to a shared object.

The way to get around this is to use Semaphores to lock the shared memory segment while a process is writing to it. (Sometimes the lock will encompass both a read and write to the shared memory, depending on what you're doing.)

Write a C Program that illustrates shared memory system calls

Method

Create a shared memory using shmget and return its ID

Using shmat attach to the segment to get a pointer to it.

Write data into the shared memory.

Detach from shared memory using shmdt.

Program

This program does one of two things: if you run it with no command line parameters, it prints the contents of the shared memory segment. If you give it one command line parameter, it stores that parameter in the shared memory segment.

Here's the Code for Shmdemo1.c:

```
#include <stdio.h>
#include <stdlib.h>
#include <string.h>
#include <sys/types.h>
#include <sys/ipc.h>
#include <sys/shm.h>
#define SHM_SIZE 1024  /* make it a 1K shared memory segment */

int main(int argc, char *argv[])
{
   key_t key;
   int shmid;
   char *data;
   int mode;

   if (argc > 2) {
      fprintf(stderr, "usage: shmdemo [data_to_write]\n");
      exit(1);
   }

   /* make the key: */
   if ((key = ftok("shmdemo1.c", 'R')) == -1) {
      perror("ftok");
      exit(1);
   }

   /* connect to (and possibly create) the segment: */
   if ((shmid = shmget(key, SHM_SIZE, 0644 | IPC_CREAT)) == -1) {
      perror("shmget");
      exit(1);
   }

   /* attach to the segment to get a pointer to it: */
   data = shmat(shmid, (void *)0, 0);
   if (data == (char *)(-1)) {
      perror("shmat");
      exit(1);
   }
```

```
  /* read or modify the segment, based on the command line: */
  if (argc == 2) {
     printf("writing to segment: \"%s\"\n", argv[1]);
     strncpy(data, argv[1], SHM_SIZE);
  } else
     printf("segment contains: \"%s\"\n", data);

  /* detach from the segment: */
  if (shmdt(data) == -1) {
     perror("shmdt");
     exit(1);
  }
  return 0;
}
```

OUTPUT

$)./shmdemol Hello

writing to segment : Hello

15. Write a C Program that illustrates inter process communication using shared memory system calls

Method

Create a shared memory using shmget and return its ID
Create a process to read from this shared memory
Using shmat attach to the segment to get a pointer to it in first process.
Write data into the shared memory.
In second process read data from the shared memory and print it
Detach from shared memory using shmdt.

6.5 Programming Examples

First compile this program and name it as shmget

```
#include<sys/shm.h>
#include<stdio.h>
#include<unistd.h>

int main(int argc, char **argv)
{
 int c,id,oflag,num;
 char *ptr;
```

```
 size_t length;
 oflag=IPC_CREAT|IPC_EXCL|0644;
 printf("enter the length\n");
 scanf("%d",&num);
 length=(long)num;
 id=shmget(ftok(argv[1],0),length,oflag);
 printf("shared memory id is %d\n",id);
 ptr=shmat(id,NULL,0);
}
```

Second compile this program and name the file as shmwrite

```
#include<sys/shm.h>
#include<stdio.h>
#include<unistd.h>
int main(int argc, char **argv)
{
 int i,id;
 unsigned char *ptr;
 struct shmid_ds buff;
 id=shmget(ftok(argv[1],0),0,0644);
 ptr=shmat(id,NULL,0);
 shmctl(id,IPC_STAT,&buff);
 for(i=0;i<buff.shm_segsz;i++)
   *ptr++ = getchar();
}
```

Third compile this program and name it as shmread

```
#include<sys/shm.h>
#include<stdio.h>
#include<unistd.h>
int main(int argc, char **argv)
{
 int i,id;
 unsigned char c,*ptr;
```

```
    struct shmid_ds buff;
    id=shmget(ftok(argv[1],0),0,0644);
    ptr=shmat(id,NULL,0);
    shmctl(id,IPC_STAT,&buff);
    for(i=0;i<buff.shm_segsz;i++)
     if(c=*ptr++)
       printf("%c\n",c);
}
```

Fourth compile this program and name it as shmrmv

```
#include<sys/types.h>
#include<sys/shm.h>
# define NULL 0
int main(int argc, char **argv)
{
  int id;
  id=shmget(ftok(argv[1],0),0,0644);
  shmctl(id,IPC_RMID,NULL);
}
```

INPUT & OUTPUT

```
as]$ ./shmget /tmp/test1
enter the length
5
shared memory id is 1310734
as]$ ipcs -m
```

------ Shared Memory Segments --------

Key	shmid	owner	perms	bytes	nattch	status
0x00000000	458764	winterscho	600	393216	2	dest
0x00000000	950285	winterscho	600	393216	2	dest
0x0006dd8e	**1310734**	winterscho	644	**5**	0	

```
as]$ ./shmwrite /tmp/test1
enter
as]$ ./shmread /tmp/test1
```

```
e
n
t
e
r
as]$ ipcs -m

------ Shared Memory Segments --------
Key          shmid     owner        perms   bytes    nattch   status
0x00000000   458764    winterscho   600     393216   2        dest
0x00000000   950285    winterscho   600     393216   2        dest
0x0006dd8e   1310734   winterscho   644     5        0

as]$ ./shmrmid /tmp/test1
as]$ ipcs -m

------ Shared Memory Segments --------
Key          shmid     owner        perms   bytes    nattch   status
0x00000000   458764    winterscho   600     393216   2        dest
0x00000000   950285    winterscho   600     393216   2        dest
```

CHAPTER 7

Message Queue

A message queue works like a FIFO, but supports some additional functionality. Generally, messages are taken off the queue in the order they are put on. Specifically, however, there are ways to pull certain messages out of the queue before they reach the front. It's like cutting in line.

In terms of usage, a process can create a new message queue, or it can connect to an existing one. When you create a message queue, it doesn't go away until you destroy it. All the processes that have ever used it can quit, but the queue will still exist. A good practice is to use the **ipcs** command to check if any of your unused message queues are just floating around out there. You can destroy them with the **ipcrm** command

7.1 How to Create a Message Queue?

To create a message queue or to get connected to message queue if it already exists use msgget() system call.

```
#include <sys/msg.h>

Int msgget(key_t key, int msgflg);
```

msgget() returns the message queue ID on success, or -1 on failure.

key is a system-wide unique identifier describing the queue you want to connect to (or create). Every other process that wants to connect to this queue will have to use the same *key*.

msgflg tells msgget() what to do with queue. To create a queue, this field must be set equal to **IPC_CREAT** bit-wise OR'd with the permissions for this queue. (The queue permissions are the same as standard file permissions--queues take on the user-id and group-id of the program that created them.)

```
#include <sys/msg.h>
key = ftok("/home/beej/somefile", 'b');
msqid = msgget(key, 0666 | IPC_CREAT);
```

In the above example, permissions on the queue are set to 666 (or rw-rw-rw).

7.2 How to send a message to the queue?

Once you've connected to the message queue using msgget(), you are ready to send and receive messages. First, the sending:

Each message is made up of two parts, which are defined in the template structure struct msgbuf, as defined in sys/msg.h:

```
struct msgbuf {
    long mtype;
    char mtext[1];
};
```

The field mtype is used later when retrieving messages from the queue, and can be set to any positive number. mtext is the data this will be added to the queue. You can use any structure you want to put messages on the queue, as long as the first element is a long. For instance, we could use this structure to store all kinds of data:

```
struct pirate_msgbuf {
    long mtype;  /* must be positive */
    char name[30];
    char ship_type;
    int notoriety;
    int cruelty;
    int booty_value;
};
```

How do we pass this information to a message queue?

Use msgsnd() system call to send messages:

```
#include <sys/msg.h>
int msgsnd(int msqid, const void *msgp, size_t msgsz, int msgflg);
```

msqid is the message queue identifier returned by msgget().

msgp is a pointer to the data you want to put on the queue.

msgsz is the size in bytes of the data to add to the queue.

msgflg allows you to set some optional flag parameters, default it can be 0.

And here is a code snippet that shows one of our pirate structures being added to the message queue:

```
#include . . .
key_t key;
int msqid;
```

```
struct pirate_msgbuf pmb = {2, "L'Olonais", 'S', 80, 10, 12035};
key = ftok("/home/beej/somefile", 'b');
msqid = msgget(key, 0666 | IPC_CREAT);
msgsnd(msqid, &pmb, sizeof(pmb), 0);  /* stick him on the queue */
```

7.3 How do we read messages from a message queue?

Use msgrcv()system call to receive messages:

```
#include <sys/msg.h>
int msgrcv(int msqid, void *msgp, size_t msgsz, long msgtyp, int msgflg);
```

Actually, the behavior of msgrcv() can be modified drastically by choosing a ***msgtyp*** that is positive, negative, or zero:

Table 1 Effects of the *msgtyp* argument on msgrcv().

msgtyp	**Effect on msgrcv()**
Zero	Retrieve the next message on the queue, regardless of its mtype.
Positive	Get the next message with an mtype **equal to** the specified *msgtyp*.
Negative	Retrieve the first message on the queue whose mtype field is less than or equal to the absolute value of the *msgtyp* argument.

A call to msgrcv() that would do it looks something like this:

```
#include

key_t key;
int msqid;
struct pirate_msgbuf pmb; /* where L'Olonais is to be kept */

key = ftok("/home/beej/somefile", 'b');
msqid = msgget(key, 0666 | IPC_CREAT);

msgrcv(msqid, &pmb, sizeof(pmb), 2, 0);  /* get him off the queue! */
```

7.4 How do we destroy a message queue?

There comes a time when you have to destroy a message queue. Like I said before, they will stick around until you explicitly remove them; it is important that you do this so that you don't waste system resources. There are two ways:

1. Use the Unix command **ipcs** to get a list of defined message queues, then use the command **ipcrm** to delete the queue.
2. Write a program to do it for you.

Often, the later choice is the most appropriate, since you might want your program to clean up the queue at some time or another. To do this requires the introduction of another function: msgctl().

The synopsis of msgctl() is:

```
#include <sys/msg.h>

int msgctl(int msqid, int cmd, struct msqid_ds *buf);
```

msqid is the queue identifier obtained from msgget().

cmd which tells msgctl() how to behave IPC_RMID, which is used to remove the message queue.

buf argument can be set to NULL for the purposes of IPC_RMID.

Say that we have the queue we created above to hold the pirates. You can destroy that queue by issuing the following call:

```
#include
.
.
msgctl(msqid, IPC_RMID, NULL);
```

Sample Program

For the sake of completeness, I'll include a brace of programs that will communicate using message queues. The first, kirk.c adds messages to the message queue, and spock.c retrieves them.

METHOD

First create a messge queue and return its ID.
From krik.c send a message to the message queue.
Read this message from spock.c from the message queue.
destroy the message queue.

7.5 Programming Examples

Here is the source for kirk.c:

```
#include <stdio.h>
#include <stdlib.h>
#include <errno.h>
```

```
#include <sys/types.h>
#include <sys/ipc.h>
#include <sys/msg.h>

struct my_msgbuf {
    long mtype;
    char mtext[200];
};
int main(void)
{
    struct my_msgbuf buf;
    int msqid;
    key_t key;

if ((key = ftok("kirk.c", 'B')) == -1) {
        perror("ftok");
        exit(1);
}
if ((msqid = msgget(key, 0644 | IPC_CREAT)) == -1) {
        perror("msgget");
        exit(1);
}
printf("Enter lines of text, ^D to quit:\n");
buf.mtype = 1; /* we don't really care message type in this case */
while(gets(buf.mtext), !feof(stdin)) {
if (msgsnd(msqid, (struct msgbuf *)&buf, sizeof(buf), 0) == -1)
        perror("msgsnd");
}
if (msgctl(msqid, IPC_RMID, NULL) == -1) {
        perror("msgctl");
        exit(1);
    }
        return 0;
}
```

The way kirk works is that it allows you to enter lines of text. Each line is bundled into a message and added to the message queue. The message queue is then read by spock.

Here is the source for spock.c:

```
#include <stdio.h>
#include <stdlib.h>
#include <errno.h>
#include <sys/types.h>
#include <sys/ipc.h>
#include <sys/msg.h>
struct my_msgbuf {
    long mtype;
    char mtext[200];
};
int main(void)
{
    struct my_msgbuf buf;
    int msqid;
    key_t key;
    if ((key = ftok("kirk.c", 'B')) == -1) {
        /* same key as kirk.c */
        perror("ftok");
        exit(1);
    }
if ((msqid = msgget(key, 0644)) == -1) {
        /* connect to the queue */
        perror("msgget");
        exit(1);
}
printf("spock: ready to receive messages, captain.\n");
for(;;) { /* Spock never quits! */
if (msgrcv(msqid, (struct msgbuf *)&buf, sizeof(buf), 0, 0) == -1)
{
        perror("msgrcv");
        exit(1);
    }
    printf("spock: \"%s\"\n", buf.mtext);
}
return 0;
}
```

Notice that spock, in the call to msgget(), doesn't include the IPC_CREAT option. We've left it up to kirk to create the message queue, and spock will return an error if he hasn't done so.

Notice what happens when you're running both in separate windows and you kill one or the other. Also try running two copies of kirk or two copies of spock to get an idea of what happens when you have two readers or two writers. Another interesting demonstration is to run kirk, enter a bunch of messages, then run spock and see it retrieve all the messages in one swoop. Just messing around with these toy programs will help you gain an understanding of what is really going on.

7.6 Conclusions

There is more to message queues than this short tutorial can present. Be sure to look in the man pages to see what else you can do, especially in the area of msgctl(). Also, there are more options you can pass to other functions to control how msgsnd() and msgrcv() handle if the queue is full or empty, respectively.

16. Write a C Program that illustrates the following,

(a) Creating a message queue.

(b) Writing to a message queue.

(c) Reading from a message queue.

Program

First compile this program and name it as msgcreat.

```
#include<sys/msg.h>
#include<stdio.h>
#include<sys/ipc.h>
#define SVMSG_MODE 0644
int main(int argc, char **argv)
{
    int c, oflag, mqid;
    oflag= IPC_CREAT|SVMSG_MODE;
    while((c=getopt(argc, argv, "e"))!=-1)
{
    switch(c)
    {
    case 'e' : oflag |= IPC_EXCL;
        break;
    }
}
```

```
if(argc != 2)
{
    printf("usage : msgcreate [-e] <pathname>");
}
mqid = msgget(ftok(argv[1],0),oflag);
printf("message created %d\n",mqid);
}
```

Second compile this program and name it as msgsend

```
#include<stdio.h>
#include<sys/msg.h>
#include<stdlib.h>
#include<sys/types.h>
#include<sys/ipc.h>
struct msgbuf
{
    long mtype;
    char mtext[1];
};

int main(int argc, char **argv)
{
    int mqid;
    size_t len;
    long type;
    struct msgbuf *ptr;
    if(argc != 4)
    {
        printf("USAGE: msgsnd <pathname> <#bytes> <type>");
    }
    else
    {
        len=atoi(argv[2]);
        type=(long)atoi(argv[3]);
        mqid=msgget(ftok(argv[1], 0),0200);

        ptr=calloc(sizeof(long) + len, sizeof(char));
        ptr->mtype = type;
```

```
        msgsnd(mqid,ptr,len,0);
        printf("message sent\n");
        exit(0);
      }
  }
```

Third compile this program and name it as msgrcv.

```
#include<stdio.h>
#include<sys/msg.h>
#include<stdlib.h>
#include<sys/types.h>
#include<sys/ipc.h>
#define MAXMSG (8192 + sizeof(long))
struct msgbuf
{
    long mtype;
    char mtext[1];
};

int main(int argc, char **argv)
{
    int mqid,c,flag,a1;
    char a;
    size_t n;
    long type;
    struct msgbuf *ptr;
    type=flag=0;
    printf("enter if you want to wait enter n for IPC_NOWAIT\n");
    a=getchar();
    if(a=='n') flag |=IPC_NOWAIT;
    printf("enter the type\n");
    scanf("%d",&a1);
    type= (long)a1;
    mqid=msgget(ftok(argv[argc-1],0),0400);
    ptr=malloc(MAXMSG);
    n=msgrcv(mqid,ptr,MAXMSG,type,flag);
    printf("read %d bytes, type= %ld\n",n,ptr->mtype);
}
```

INPUT & OUTPUT

```
as]$ touch /tmp/test2
as]$ ./msgcreate /tmp/test2
message created 65538
as]$ ./msgsnd /tmp/test2 1 100
message sent
as]$ ./msgsnd /tmp/test2 2 200
message sent
as]$ ./msgsnd /tmp/test2 3 300
message sent
as]$ ipcs -q

------ Message Queues --------
Key           msqid    owner         perms    used-bytes    messages
0x0006dd8f    65538    winterscho    644      6             3

/* to display the details of message queue*/
as]$ ipcs -qu

------ Messages: Status --------
allocated queues = 3
used headers = 3
used space = 6 bytes

as]$ ipcs -qt
------ Message Queues Send/Recv/Change Times --------
msqid     owner         send               recv       change
65538     winterscho    Mar 30 03:56:17    Not set    Mar 30 03:55:34

as]$ ipcs -qp

------ Message Queues PIDs --------
Msqid     owner         lspid    lrpid
65538     winterscho    3315     0

as]$ ipcs -qc

------ Message Queues: Creators/Owners --------
msqid    perms    cuid            cgid            uid             gid
65538    644      winterschool    winterschool    winterschool    winterschool
```

```
as]$ ./msgrcv /tmp/test2
enter if you want to wait enter n for IPC_NOWAIT
n
enter the type
100
read 1 bytes, type= 100
as]$ ./msgrcv /tmp/test2
enter if you want to wait enter n for IPC_NOWAIT
n
enter the type
-300
read 2 bytes, type= 200
as]$ ./msgsnd /tmp/test2 5 500
message sent
as]$ ./msgrcv /tmp/test2
enter if you want to wait enter n for IPC_NOWAIT
n
enter the type
500
read 5 bytes, type= 500
as]$ ./msgrcv /tmp/test2
enter if you want to wait enter n for IPC_NOWAIT
x
enter the type
300
read 3 bytes, type= 300

/* blocked as there are no messages in the queue */

as]$ ./msgrcv /tmp/test2
enter if you want to wait enter n for IPC_NOWAIT
x
enter the type
300

[2]+  Stopped                 ./msgrcv /tmp/test2
as]$ ./msgrcv /tmp/test2
enter if you want to wait enter n for IPC_NOWAIT
n
```

enter the type
300
read -1 bytes, type= 0 /* not blocked but returns -1 bytes */
as]$

as]$ ipcs -qu

------ Messages: Status --------
allocated queues = 3
used headers = 0
used space = 0 bytes

as]$ ipcs -q

------ Message Queues --------

key	msqid	owner	perms	used-bytes	messages
0x0006dd8f	**65538**	winterscho	644	0	0

as]$ **ipcrm -q 65538**
as]$ ipcs -q

------ Message Queues --------
key msqid owner perms used-bytes messages

Exercises

Create the following database file as emp.txt and use : as separator for each field and execute the following queries:

EMPNO	ENAME	JOB	MGR	HIREDATE	SALARY	COMM	DEPTNO
7499	ALLEN	SALESMAN	7698	20/FEB/81	1700	300	30
7521	WARD	SALESMAN	7698	22/FEB/81	1350	500	30
7566	JONES	MANAGER	7839	02/APR/81	3075	0	20
7654	MARTIN	SALESMAN	7698	28/SEP/81	1350	1400	30
7698	BLAKE	MANAGER	7839	01/MAY/81	2950	0	30
7782	CLARK	MANAGER	7839	09/JUN/81	4100	0	10
7788	SCOTT	ANALYST	7566	19/APR/87	4100	0	20
7839	KING	PRESIDENT	-	17/NOV/81	6300	0	20
7844	TURNER	SALESMAN	7698	08/SEP/81	1600	0	30
7876	ADAMS	CLERK	7788	23/MAY/87	5200	0	20
7900	JAMES	CLERK	7788	23/DEC/87	5050	0	30
7902	FORD	ANALYST	7566	03/DEC/81	3100	0	20
7934	MILLER	CLERK	7782	23/JAN/82	6600	0	10

1. Display the list of names of employees working in department no 30

   cut –d : -f 2,8 emp.txt | grep '30'|cut –d: -f 1

2. Display the employees working under the manager 7698

   cut –d : -f 2,4 emp.txt | grep '7698'|cut –d: -f 1

3. Display all salespersons

   cut –d : -f 2,3 emp.txt | grep 'SALESMAN'|cut –d: -f 1

4. Display the employees who joined in the month of February

   cut –d : -f 2,5 emp.txt | grep '/FEB/'|cut –d: -f 1

5. Display the employees as per the dictionary order

   cut –d : -f 2 emp.txt | sort

6. Display the employees list in reverse order

   cut –d : -f 2 emp.txt | sort -r

7. Create another file with same data.

   cp emp.txt emp1.txt

8. Merge both files and print the unique department number.

   sort –u `cut –d: -f 8 emp.txt` `cut –d: -f 8 emp1.txt`

9. Display the hiredate, salary, department of President.

   cut –d: -f 3,5,6,8 emp.txt | grep 'PRESIDENT'

10. Display the employees list working in department 10 and 20 in alphabetical order.

    cut –d : -f 2,8 emp.txt | grep '[23]0'|cut –d: -f 1 |sort

11. Display the employees list whose name starts with A.

    cut –d : -f 2 emp.txt | grep '^A'

12. Display the employees list whose names do not start with A

    cut –d : -f 2 emp.txt | grep '[^A]'

13. Display the employee file content 5 lines at a time

14. With out using cp command, write the contents of this file to another.

    cat emp.txt > emp1.txt

15. Write a command which writes the name of president in large letters.

    cut –d: -f 2,3 emp.txt | grep 'PRESIDENT' |cut –d; -f 1| banner

    Note: (banner works unix environment)

16. Write a command which display the number of people working under any one manager

    cut –d : -f 2,4 emp.txt | grep '7698'|cut –d: -f 1 |wc -l

17. Display only the employee name, hiredate and department number

    cut –d: -f 2,5,8 emp.txt

18. List all the files that are directories and that do not have execution permission

    ls –l | grep '^d[r-][w-]-[r-][w-]-[r-][w-]-'

19. Display the number of distinct jobs

    cut –d : -f 3 emp.txt | sort -u

20. Find the date of joining of all employees

    cut –d : -f 2,5 emp.txt

21. Write a command that reads first 10 lines and finds the list of salesperson and print their names.

    head -10 emp.txt | grep 'SALESMAN' | cut –d: -f 2

22. List the names of employees starting with vowels.

    cut –d : -f 2 emp.txt |grep '^[AEIOUaeiou]'

23. List the names of employees not starting with a vowel.

    cut –d : -f 2 emp.txt |grep '[^AEIOUaeiou]'

24. Write a command that creates a new file which contains the data same as old file but with all small case letters.

    tr '[A-Z]' '[a-z]' emp.txt >emp1.txt

25. Write a command to display the number of digits used for empno.

    cut –d: -f 1 emp.txt| head -1 |wc -c

26. Write a command to list out all the system process.

    ps –ax

Assignment for Shell Scripts

1. Write a shell program to calculate the salary based on the following fact.

   If basic salary < 1500 then HRA = 10% of basic salary

   DA = 90% " "

   If basic salary >= 1500 then HRA = 500

   DA = 98%

2. Read a file and if the file has write permission then append the text given through keyboard to the file at the beginning
3. Check whether the file has all permissions if it is a file, if directory, list the contents of directory, if filename not given display the comments.
4. Read a single digit number and display in words.
5. Get the information of the current user and based on this information list all processes of that user.
6. Read a word and display whether it starts with vowel / consonant / digit / special character.
7. Write a shell script which gets displayed the message "GM/GA/GE " depend upon the current time.
8. Write a program which reads data from a file and prints on a console.
9. Write a program that either reads from a file or from keyboard and counts no of lines and words.
10. Write a program to check whether user has logged in or not.
11. Write a program which prints largest of 10 numbers given as arguments or through keyboard.
12. Write a program to find the factorial value of any number entered through the keyboard.
13. Write shell script which works similar to the following unix commands head, tail, more

14. Write a program which gives permissions to all files specified in a directory/Sub directory given its path as argument.
15. Write a program which takes contents of current directory and if it is a file take an argument from keyboard to sort / cat and based on that execute that command.
16. Write a shell script which reads two integers and two float numbers and apply +, –, * , / on them and displays the result.
17. Write a shell script which checks whether the given name is file or directory.
18. Write a shell script which displays the exit status of any command which is given as command argument.
19. Write a shell script which reads a number between 0 and 9 and displays it in words using if.
20. Write a shell script which reads marks in 5 different subjects through key board and give the division as,

    first if marks are > 60

    second if marks are between 50-59

    third if marks are between 40-49

    Fail if marks are less than 40
21. Write a shell script which works similar to ls command which lists all the files that are starting with a specific character.
22. Write a shell script to create 4 directories in the current directory and in each directory create two subdirectories and in each sub directory create two files f1 & f2.
23. Write a shell script which works as bash shell i.e., it should take a command and execute it until you logout.

Assignment on Files

1. Write a program, which creates file with given name and writes the byte values from 0 to 0xff. The program closes the file and returns.

   Now try to open the file created in the above step, using the vi editor. What do you expect to see?
2. Write a program which closes the standard input file descriptor, opens a given file. Dups this file to the standard input. Reads the standard input one line at a time. Displays till end of file is encountered.
3. Write a program which closes the standard output file descriptor , opens a given file. Dups this file to the standard output. Each of these lines is get from the gets() system call.
4. Write a program which reads the contents of the file in reverse order.
5. Write a program which creates holes in a file and copy the entire contents to another file and also display on the console.
6. Write a program which replaces the occurrence of 'GNITS' to 'gnits' in a file.

Assignment on Processes and Signals

1. Write a program to install the exit handler, in the exit handler function just print a statement. Try to install more than one exit handler.
2. Write a program to get and print the following process identifiers.

   Process Id, Parent process id, user id, effective user id, group id and effective group id.
3. Write a "hello world\n" program. Write a separate program, which runs the hello world program using 'execv' system call.
4. Write a program to catch the SIGINT signal. In the main program use pause() signal in a for loop for 5 times. In the signal handler print "I caught the SIGINT signal".
5. Install a signal handler for alarm signal. Next take sleep time from the user and give alarm() with the given number of seconds. Now use pause to wait for signal.

   Print a message for alarm signal handler.

Viva Questions for Shell Commands

1. Which command is used for searching a pattern in a file?

   Using grep command
2. What are the different types of shells available in unix?

   bourne shell, korn shell, C shell, bash shell
3. What does a sticky bit for a directory and an executable file signify?

   sticky bit can be set to regular files which enables the program to be loaded in fixed locations ex : vi editor & emacs editor
4. State two different ways in which we can identify whether a given file is an ordinary file or a directory?

   When listed using ls –l the file type bit is set to d and nuber of links is 2 by default.
5. What is the meaning of '.' and '..'?

   '.' refers to current directory and '..' refers to parent directory.
6. How will you forcibly remove a file to which you don't have write permission?

   Using rm command with –f option
7. What information does a super block contain?

   Contains global information about disk usage and availiability of data blocks and inodes.
8. Can a file have more than two links?

   Yes.

9. Can a file has links across file systems?

   we can have hard links within a file system and soft links/symbolic links across different file system.

10. Does the df command report the free disk space in bytes?

    df command reports the free disk space for each file system in terms of blocks.

11. How would you find out how much space is used by the directory /usr/cse100/mydir?

    Use du command

12. If a file occupies 10 blocks on the disk is it guaranteed that these blocks would be in adjacent locations on the disk?

    No

13. What are the four components of a Unix file system?

    Boot block, super block, inode blocs, and data block

14. What is a filter? name some.

    Filter reads from standard input and writes to standard output. Ex: grep, cut , wc, sort, etc.

15. Can we change the modification time of a file without using cat/ chmod options?

    Using touch command with –a option.

16. What do the term UID, PID, PPID stand for? For a particular process which is currently executing how can you obtain these values?

    UID user identification, PID process identification PPID parent process identification. use getuid(), getpid(), getppid() methods to get the information.

17. How will you terminate a process which has gone in an infinite loop?

    Using kill command

18. If the nice value of a process is increased, what would be the effect on the speed of execution of the process?

    If nice value is increased then the priority of the process is decreased and the process may take long time for execution.

19. Where would be the output of the command " nohup sort aaa bbb ccc stored?

    Allows the sort command to run even after the user has logged out.

20. Which process cannot be killed using KILL command?

    System process.

21. How will you find out which jobs have been submitted for execution?

    Using ps command

22. What is the difference between scheduling process using batch command and using at command?

    Batch command schedules the jobs and are executed as soon as the system load permits. At command schedules and executes the jobs depending on the time specified.

23. Can you run a shell script once it has been typed?

    It should have execution permissions.

24. What is the difference between expr and bc command?

    exper command performs arithmetic operations on intigers and string manipulations.

    bc command performs all arithmetic operations, conversions, scientific calculations.

25. How can you get the set of arguments passed at command line arguments?

    Using positional parameters

Viva Questions for File Handling Utilities

1. What is maximum size of file that can be allowed for any file?

   2 GB on 32 bit machine

2. How can you limit the size of file?

   Using ulimit command

3. Can we set the permissions to a file using open function?

   Yes

4. What is the difference between read and scanf function?

   Read is a low level system call and scanf is a standard I/O function

5. Using read can we read from a file? If so how?

   Yes, using file descriptor

6. Name the system call that duplicates the file descriptor?

   dup & dup2

7. What is atomic operation?

   Performing two or more critical operations in atomic manner.

8. Can we dup the file descriptor without using dup or dup2 functions?

   Yes, using fcntl function.

9. How can you change the permissions of the file that is already open?

   Using chmod function

10. How can you position the file descriptor at the required position?

    Using dup2 function

11. What are the options of whence argument in lseek function? What do they signify?

    To set the descriptor at bigining or at the end or at any place from the current position.

12. Name the library file to be included to use the constants for permissions?

    sys/types.h

13. Is duplication of file descriptor using fcntl is automic?
    Yes
14. How many types of buffering scheme is available in UNIX?
    full buffered, line buffered and unbuffered
15. What is the difference between line buffer and full buffer?
    line buffer writes to file at the end of every line and full buffer writes when the buffer is full or when the operation is complete.
16. How many data structures are maintained by the kernel with respective to the opened files? What are they?
    stat structure is maintained by the kernel when a file is opened

Viva Questions for Process & Signals

1. What is a process?
   Program in execution.
2. In how many modes a process can run?
   2 modes
3. What is the difference between the process running in user mode and in kernel mode?
   When it is in kernel mode it has all privileges to access the resources which is not possible when it is in user mode.
4. what is context switching?
   switching from one process to other.
5. How many states can a process have? What are those?
   5 states–new, ready, execution, blocked and halt states
6. What are Zombies?
   The process whose termination status is not received by the parent process
7. How can you create a process in the running process?
   Using fork() method.
8. How many times fork() return? With what values?
   Two times returning 0 in child process and pid of child process in parent process
9. What is the difference between fork() and vfork()?
   In fork() either child or parent process can start. In vfork() parent process starts after the child process calls exec to swap with new process.
10. Can we run a different process in the current process? So what happens if a new process is started on the current process?
    Using exec command, when new process is started it does not return back.
11. What are different ways a process can terminate?
    Normal termination and abnormal termination.

12. What is difference between normal termination and abnormal termination?

    In normal termination the exit status is send to the parent process which is not possible in abnormal termination.

13. How can a parent process get the termination details of its child process?

    Using wait method

14. what is the difference between wait() and waitpid()?

    wait method waits until any first process terminates. waitpid() waits for a particular process to terminate.

15. What is exit handler?

    It is a special method to be executed when the process terminates.

16. How can you register an exit handler?

    Using atexit method

17. What happens when an exit handler is registered and the program terminates using _exit()?

    exit handler is not invoked.

18. What is the significance of exec? How many options of exec are available?

    To swap the current process with new process. There are 6 forms of exec.

19. What is the difference between execv and execl?

    execv takes the argument vector and execl takes the list of arguments.

20. What is the difference between execvp and execlp?

    These two functions take the path of the executable file. The arguments to be passed varies depending on the function name. execvp requires the address of the vector containing the arguments. execlp requires the list of arguments to be specified followed by a null pointer.

21. What is the difference between execve and execle?

    execve takes the argument vector and execle takes the list of arguments and both takes the environment in which it has to execute.

22. Which form of exec is the system call?

    execve

23. Name the system call which executes a new process and stays in the current process?

    system()

24. What is a signal handler?

    It is a special function that is invoked when a particular signal is generated.

25. How can you register a signal handler?

    Using signal() method.

26. What is signal delay?

    It is the difference time between the generation of signal and its handling.

27. Name the signals that cannot be ignored?

    SIGINT, SIGTERM etc

28. What is reliable signal?

    Once a signal handler is register any number of times that signal is generated it is handled by signal handler.

29. Name the signals that are generated with kill command?

    SIGTERM

30. Arithmetic exceptions cause the generation of which signal?

    SIGFPE

31. When is the signal SIGINT generated?

    When ctrl _c is pressed.

32. What is difference between pause() and alarm()?

    pause cause the process to block until alarm awakes the blocked process.

33. What is difference between sleep() and pause()?

    sleep causes the process to be suspended for the specified time. pause suspends indefinetly.

34. What is the significance of raise() function?

    It is used to raise the required signal.

35. What is unreliable signal?

    signals are unreliable if they perform default action after it is handled once.

36. How can you make an unreliable signal as reliable?

    Reregister it again in the signal handler.

Viva Questions for Record Locking

1. What is file lock/ record lock?

   lock applied on complete file is file lock. lock applied on a single record is record lock.

2. What is shared lock?

   read-write lock for reading is called shared lock.

3. What is exclusive lock?

   read-write lock for writing is called exclusive lock.

4. What information is stored in lock structure?

   Type of lock, whence, start position, length of lock, the process id which gained the lock.

5. What is the purpose of F_GETLK command used in fcntl function?

   To test if lock is applied on the specified region.

6. What is the purpose of F_SETLK command used in fcntl function?

   To set lock on the specified region.

7. Can we lock the region of the file which is more than the size of the file?

   Yes, for writing.

8. When the region is already locked in read mode, what happens when a request comes to gain read lock?

   granted.

9. When the region is already locked in write mode, what happens when a request comes to gain read lock?

   blocked.

10. Name the library files to be included to apply the locks of the files?

    fcntl.h,

Viva Questions for IPC

1. What is inter process communication?

   Communication between different process using pipes, message queues, shared memory is IPC.

2. What are pipes?

   It is a communication channel between related process with one way data flow.

3. Can we have two way communication using a single pipe?

   No

4. How many descriptors are there for a single pipe?

   Two descriptors

5. How pipes are different from FIFO's?

   pipes are used between two related process, FIFO can be used between two processes, which has common parent.

6. Can a single process use a pipe?

   It is meaning less.

7. Which sequence is appropriate to have IPC using pipe? Fork followed by pipe / pipe followed by fork?

   pipe followed by fork.

8. To have two way communications between two process how many pipes are required?

   Two pipes

9. What are named pipes?

   FIFO

10. What happens when you read from a FIFO when the write end is not in use?
    reading gets blocked.
11. Who maintains the IPC structure? What is the use of IPC structure?
    ipc_perm structure maintains information of each IPC object.
12. How can you create a key?
    Using ftok() function
13. Can we create an IPC object without ftok function?
    Using IPC_PRIVATE option
14. What are the arguments required for creating an object using XXXget()?
    key for assigning unique ID, oflag for specifying read-write permissions.
15. Is it true that always using msgget() function it creates a message queue?
    No, only once for each key.
16. Name the commands that are used for finding the information of the IPC objects?
    ipcs
17. Name the command that is used for deleting the IPC object?
    Ipcrm
18. What is a semaphore?
    It is a primitive used to provide synchronization between various processes.
19. What is the difference between binary semaphore and count semaphore?
    binary semaphore is meant for a single resource and count semaphore can handle more than one resource.
20. What is the significance of using IPC_NOWAIT?
    When a call is maid to use a resource which is busy then the call gets blocked to avoid blocking of the system call IPC_NOWAIT is used.
21. Among all IPC which is the fastest means of communication?
    shared memory
22. Can the shared memory be used by the processes that are unrelated?
    yes.
23. Can we define a semaphore for a shared memory?
    yes
24. Can we make a selection of the message that can be read?
    Yes, if we create a int pointer it reads integer data, if it is char pointer then it can be used to read characters, and so on.
25. Name the reliable means of communication?
    message queue

26. What is the life time of pipe?

    Until the processes are active.

27. What is the life time of FIFO?

    Until it is physically removed.

28. What is the life time of message queue?

    Until it is physically removed.

29. To use functions related to message queue which header files have to be included?

    sys/msg.h

30. To use functions related to semaphores which header files have to be included?

    sys/sem.h

31. To use functions related to shared memory which header files have to be included?

    sys/shm.h

32. To have parent to child communication which set of descriptors of pipe have to be closed?

    read descriptor of parent and write descriptor of child should be closed.

33. To have two way communication between parent and child which kind of IPC is best?

    pipes

34. To have two way communication between server and client which kind of IPC is suitable?

    message queues

Part - II

Compiler Design

Introduction to Compiler

A compiler is a program that reads a program in one language, the source language and translates into an equivalent program in another language, the target language.

The translation process should also report the presence of errors in the source program.

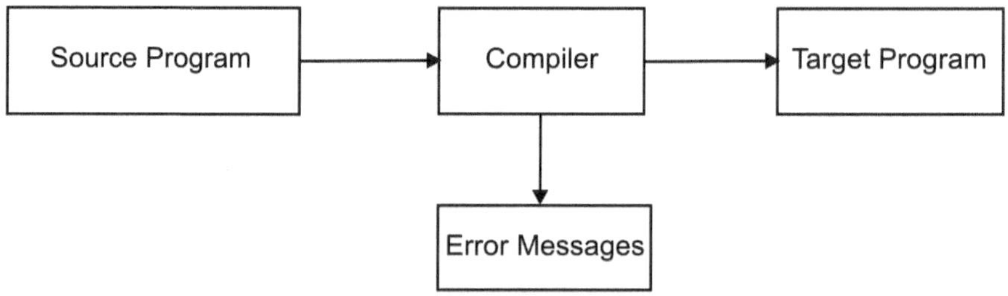

There are Two Parts of Compilation

The analysis part breaks up in the source program into constant piece and creates an intermediate representation of the source program.

The synthesis part constructs the desired target program from the intermediate representation.

Phases of Compiler

The compiler design is divided into 6 phases.

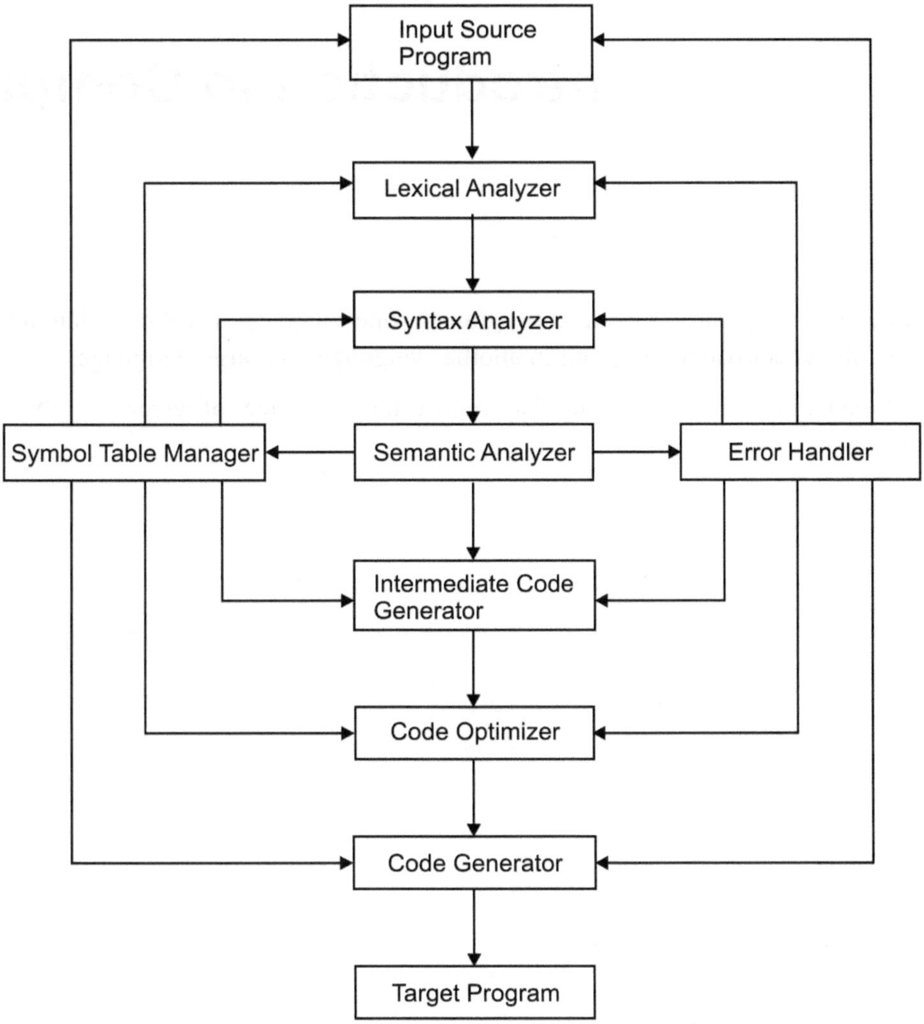

The cousins of the compiler are

1. Preprocessor.
2. Assembler.
3. Loader and Link-editor.

Front End vs Back End: The phases of a compiler are collected into front end and back end.

The front end includes all analysis phases end the intermediate code generator.

The back end includes the code optimization phase and final code generation phase.

The front end analyzes the source program and produces intermediate code while the back end synthesizes the target program from the intermediate code.

1. Lexical analyzer takes the source program as an input and produces a long string of tokens.
2. Syntax Analyzer takes an out of lexical analyzer and produces a large tree.
3. Semantic analyzer takes the output of syntax analyzer and produces another tree.
4. Similarly, intermediate code generator takes a tree as an input produced by semantic analyzer and produces intermediate code.
5. Code optimizer optimizes the code to improve the efficiency.
6. Target code generator produces machine code.

Draw Backs of Design

- Requires enormous amount of space to store tokens and trees.
- Very slow since each phase would have to input and output to and from temporary disk

Remedy

- Use syntax directed translation to inter leaves the actions of phases.
- Compiler construction tools.

Compiler Construction Tools

Parser Generators: The specification of input based on regular expression. The organization is based on finite automation.

Scanner Generator: The specification of input based on regular expression. The organization is based on finite automation.

Syntax-Directed Translation: It walks the parse tee and as a result generate intermediate code.

Automatic Code Generators: Translates intermediate rampage into machine language.

Data-Flow Engines: It does code optimization using data-flow analysis.

CHAPTER 8

Lexical Analysis

8.1 Introduction

Lexical Analysis is the act of breaking down source code into a set of lexemes. Each lexeme is found by matching sequential characters to a token.

Lexical Analysis can be performed with pattern matching through the use of Regular Expressions. Therefore, a Lexical Analyzer can be defined and represented as a DFA.

Even though the source language is likely written as Context Free, the Lexical Analyzer identifies strings and sends them to a Syntax Analyzer for parsing. The Lexical Analyzer will remove white space, comments, and identify ill-formed strings or invalid characters.

Reasons to Separate Lexical Analysis from Syntax Analysis

1. *Simplicity:* Techniques for Lexical Analysis can be simpler than those required for Syntax Analysis. DFA vs. PDA. Separation also simplifies the Syntax Analyzer.
2. *Efficiency:* Separation into different modules makes it easier to perform simplifications and optimizations unique to the different paradigms.
3. *Portability:* Due to input/output and character set variations, Lexical Analyzers are not always machine independent.

Errors often detected in a lexical analyzer

1. Numeric literals those are too long.
2. Identifiers that are too long (often a warning is given)
3. Ill-formed numeric literals.
4. Input characters that are not in the source language

8.2 Example of a Lexical Analyzer

Suppose that we want to build a lexical analyzer for the REs:

For-keyword = for

identifier = [a-z][a-z0-9]*

The corresponding DFA that recognizes the above tokens has 4 final states: one to accept the *for-keyword* and 3 to accept an identifier:

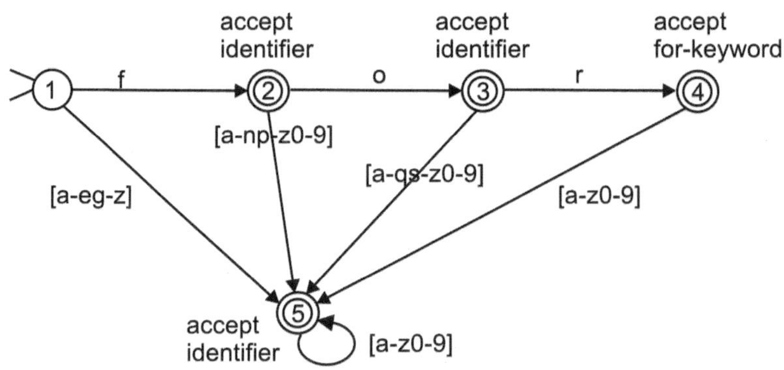

Another Example

Build a Lexical Analyzer which identifies the following tokens:

1. digits
2. digits E [sign] digits
3. digits.digits [E [sign] digits]

   "sign" refers to +,-

   "E" refers to exponent by power 10

   [ ] refers to 0 or 1 of contents

   { } refers to 0 or more of contents

   $\acute{\varepsilon} = \lambda$

The above tokens can be accepted by the following DFA

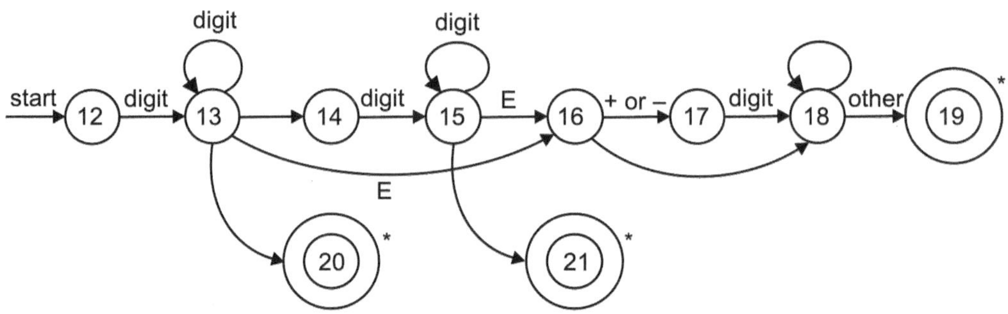

Approaches to constructing a Lexical Analyzer

1. Write hand code.
2. Use lex tool.

8.2(a) Program & Logic

Design a Lexical analyzer in C language for the below language. The lexical analyzer should ignore redundant spaces, tabs and newlines. It should also ignore comments. Although the syntax specification states that identifiers can be arbitrarily long, you may restrict the length to some reasonable value,

- **Read following code in file input.dat**

```
main()
{
    int a,b;
    if ( a > b )
        printf("hai");
else
        b=100; /* this is comment */
}
```

- **Read text line by line and each line character by character and divide it into different words.**
- **Match words with tokens like num, id, keyword, opr etc.**
- **To distinguish between keyword and id, compare word with keywords first, if it does not match then treat it as id.**
- **Print token along with lexeme and line number.**

8.2 (b) Lexical Analyzer Coding in C Language

```
/* Lexical Analyzer for any C program as input */

#include<stdio.h>
#include<string.h>
void main()
{
 int l,i,j,k,m;
 char *c[5]={"print","int","then","endif","if"};
 char temp[100]={0} ,str[20];
 FILE *fp;
 clrscr();
 fp=fopen("input.dat","r");                /* input file */
 printf("Lexeme   Token   Line no.\n");    /* Out put format */
 for(l=1;!feof(fp);l++)
 {
```

```
fgets(temp,100,fp);
for(i=0;temp[i]!='\0';)
{
 if(temp[i]==' ')                          /* skip spaces */
  i++;
 else if(temp[i]=='\n')
  temp[i]='\0';
 else if(isalpha(temp[i]))
 {
 j=0;
  while(isalnum(temp[i]))
  {
   str[j]=temp[i];
   j++;
   i++;
  }                                        /*  recognizing arrays */
  if(temp[i]=='[')
  {
   str[j]='\0';
   printf("%s      array    %d\n",str,l);
   i++; j=0;
   while(temp[i]!=']')
   {
    str[j]=temp[i];
    j++;
    i++;
   }
   str[j]='\0';
   printf("%s      index   %d\n",str,l);
   i++;
  }
  else                                     /* check for  keyword or id */
  {

  str[j]='\0';
  for(k=0;k<5;k++)
  {
```

```
 if(!strcmp(c[k],str))
  break;
 }
 if(k==5)
  printf("%s   identifier  %d\n",str,l);
 else
  printf("%s   keyword    %d\n",str,l);
 }
}                                          /* check for Number */

else if(isdigit(temp[i]))
{
j=0;
 while(isdigit(temp[i]))
 {
  str[j]=temp[i];
  j++;
  i++;
 }
 str[j]='\0';
 printf("%s   key const   %d\n",str,l);
}                                          /* check for comment lines */

else if((temp[i]=='/')&&(temp[i+1]=='*'))
{
 printf("/* start of  comment  %d\n",l);
 i=i+2;
 while(temp[i]!='*' && temp[i+1]!='/'&&temp[i]!='\n')
 {
  i=i+1;
  if(temp[i]=='\n')
  {
   fgets(temp,100,fp);
   l++;
  }
 }
  i=i+2;
```

```
 printf("*/end of comment  %d\n",l);
}                                          /* check for operator */

else
{
 j=0;
 str[j]=temp[i];
 j++;
 switch(temp[i])
 {
  case '+':
  case '-':
  case '*':
  case '/':
  case '=':
  case '>':
  case '<':
  case '<=':
  case '>=':
  case '%':{
        if(temp[i]=='%'&&(temp[i+1]=='d'||temp[i+1]=='f'||temp[i+1]=='c'))
        {
      str[j]=temp[++i];
      i++;j++;
      str[j]='\0';
      printf("%s  specialsymbol %d \n ",str,l);
      j=0;
       break;
        }
        else
        {
      str[j]='\0';
      printf("%s   operator  %d\n",str,l);
      j=0;
      i++;  break;
        }
       }
```

```
        case '(':
        case ')':
        case '{':
        case '}':{
              str[j]='\0';
              printf("%s   paranthesis  %d\n",str,l);
              j=0;
              i++;
              break;
              }
        case ';':{
              str[j]='\0';
              printf("%s   punct symbol  %d\n",str,l);
              j=0;
              i++;
              break;
              }
        default:{
             str[j]='\0';
             j=0;
             i++;
             printf("%s   specialsymbol  %d\n",str,l);
             break;
             }
        }
      }
    }
  }
  getch();
}
```

8.2 (C) Results

Lexeme	Token	Line no
main	keyword	1
(	parenthesis	1
)	parenthesis	1
{	parenthesis	2

int	keyword	3
a	identifier	3
,	special symbol	3
b	identifier	3
;	punct symbol	3
if	keyword	4
(	parenthesis	4
a	identifier	4
>	operator	4
b	identifier	4
)	parenthesis	4
printf	keyword	5
(	parenthesis	5
“	punct symbol	5
hai	identifier	5
”	punct symbol	5
)	parenthesis	5
;	punct symbol	5
else	keyword	6
b	identifier	7
=	operator	7
100	keyconst	7
;	punct symbol	7
/* this is comment */	comment	7
}	parenthesis	8

8.3 Viva Questions

1. What is the role of a Lexical analyzer in compilation process?

   Lexical analyzer reads source text and divides them in to stream of tokens.

2. Define the terms: tokens, Pattern and Lexeme.

   Token is group of characters with logical meaning.

   Pattern is rule that describes a token. Usually a regular expression.

Lexeme is actual text that matches the pattern and is recognized as token

Ex: pi = 3.1416

Token	lexeme	pattern
id	pi	letter(letter|digit)*
assign	=	=
num	3.1416	Numeric constant

3. Give example of lexical error

   $xyz – identifier does not start with $.

4. Give examples of nontokens in C program

   #include, #define, /*

5. Write regular expressions for patterns integer numbers and real numbers with scientific notation.

   Let D is [0-9]*

   Real number is D+(.D+)?(E(+|-)?D+)

6. What are other tasks performed by Lexical analyzer other than dividing text to tokens.

   Removes Comment lines and white space characters

   Correlates error messages.

7. Can we combine Lexical analysis phase with Parsing? If not why?

   Yes, if the source language is too simple. But the advantage of having as a separate phase is that design in simplified and we can use automated tools.

8. What are the error recovery strategies used by Lexical analyzer?

   Panic mode error recovery.

   Deleting an extra character

   Inserting a missing character

9. What are the advantages of having Lexical analysis as a separate phase?

   Simplifies the design of compiler

   Increases efficiency of compiler

   Improves the portability of compiler

10. Find the number of tokens in following code

    if (x > y) . z=0;

    10

8.4 Exercises

(a) Run the lexical analyzer for the following C program and comment on tokens/output

```
main()
{ int a[3],t1,t2;
t1=2;
a[0]=1; a[1]=2; a[t1]=3;
t2 = -(a[2]+t1*6)/(a[2]-t1);
if t2>5 then
print(t2);
else{
int t3;
t3=99;
t2=-25;
print(-t1 +t2*t3); /*this is a comment on 2 lines */
} endif }
```

(b) Write a program for lexical analyzer to divide the following C program to tokens.

```
main()
{
int x,y,z;
x=10;
y=20;
z=30;
}
```

(c) Run the lexical analyzer for the following C program and comment on tokens/output.

```
   main()
{
    int i,j,t;
    for(i=0;i<10;i++)
        t=t+10;
}
```

(d) Run the lexical analyzer for the following C program and comment on tokens/output.

```
main()
{
int i,j;
while(i<100)
   {
   i=i+10;
   printf("%d\n",&i);
   }
}
```

CHAPTER 9

Lex Tool

9.1 Introduction

Lex is a program generator designed for lexical processing of character input streams. It accepts a high-level, problem oriented specification for character string matching, and produces a program in a general purpose language which recognizes regular expressions.

The regular expressions are specified by the user in the source specifications given to Lex. The Lex written code recognizes these expressions in an input stream and partitions the input stream into strings matching the expressions. At the boundaries between strings program sections provided by the user are executed. The Lex source file associates the regular expressions and the program fragments. As each expression appears in the input to the program written by Lex, the corresponding fragment is executed.

The user supplies the additional code beyond expression matching needed to complete his tasks, possibly including code written by other generators. Lex itself exists on UNIX, GCOS, and OS/370; but the code generated by Lex may be taken anywhere the appropriate compilers exist.

Lex turns the user's expressions and actions (called *source* in this Memo) into the host general-purpose language; the generated program is named *yylex.* The *yylex* program will recognize expressions in a stream (called *input* in this Memo) and perform the specified actions for each expression as it is declared in translation schema. See Figure 9.1.

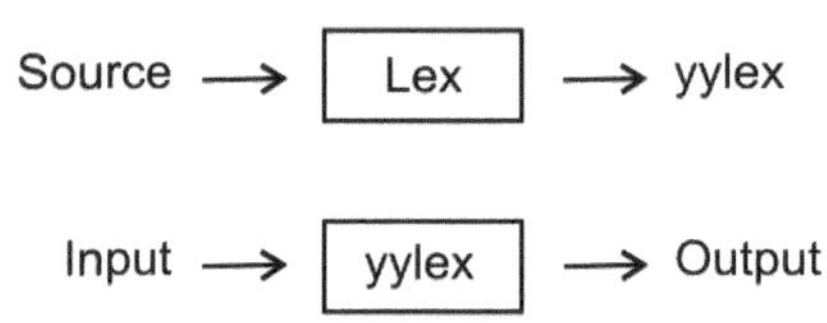

Fig 9.1 An overview of Lex.

For a trivial example, consider a program to delete from the input all blanks or tabs at the ends of lines.

```
%%
[ \t]+$ ;
```

is all that is required. The program contains a %% delimiter to mark the beginning of the rules, and one rule. This rule contains a regular expression which matches one or more instances of the characters blank or tab (written \t for visibility, in accordance with the C language convention) just prior to the end of a line. The brackets indicate the character class made of blank and tab; the + indicates ''one or more ...''; and the $ indicates ''end of line,'' as in QED. No action is specified, so the program generated by Lex (yylex) will ignore these characters. Everything else will be copied. To change any remaining string of blanks or tabs to a single blank, add another rule:

```
%%
[ \t]+$ ;
[ \t]+ printf(" ");
```

The finite automaton generated for this source will scan for both rules at once, observing at the termination of the string of blanks or tabs whether or not there is a new line character, and executing the desired rule action. The first rule matches all strings of blanks or tabs at the end of lines, and the second rule all remaining strings of blanks or tabs. Lex can be used alone for simple transformations, or for analysis and statistics gathering on a lexical level. Lex generates a deterministic finite automaton from the regular expressions in the source. The automaton is interpreted, rather than compiled, in order to save space. The result is still a fast analyzer. In particular, the time taken by a Lex program to recognize and partition an input stream is proportional to the length of the input. Lex is not limited to source which can be interpreted on the basis of one character look ahead.

For example, if there are two rules, one looking for *ab* and another for *abcdefg*, and the input stream is *abcdefh*, Lex will recognize *ab* and leave the input pointer just before *cd.* Such backup is more costly than the processing of simpler languages.

Lex Source

The general format of Lex source is:

```
{definitions}
%%
{rules}
%%
{user subroutines}
```

The definitions and the user subroutines are often omitted. The second *%%* is optional, but the first is required to mark the beginning of the rules. The absolute minimum Lex program is thus

```
%%
(no definitions, no rules)
```

which translates into a program which copies the input to the output unchanged. In the outline of Lex programs shown above, the *rules* represent the user's control decisions; they are a table, in which the left column contains *regular expressions* and the right column contains *actions,* program fragments to be executed when the expressions are recognized. Thus an individual rule might appear integer printf("found keyword INT");to look for the string *integer* in the input stream and print the message ''found keyword INT'' whenever it appears. In this example the host procedural language is C and the C library function *printf* is used to print the string. The end of the expression is indicated by the first blank or tab character. If the action is merely a single C expression, it can just be given on the right side of the line; if it is compound, or takes more than a line, it should be enclosed in braces. As a slightly more useful example, suppose it is desired to change a number of words from British to American spelling. Lex rules such as

```
colour printf("color");
mechanise printf("mechanize");
petrol printf("gas");
```

would be a start. These rules are not quite enough, since the word *petroleum* would become *gaseum*;

Lex Regular Expressions

Regular expressions in Lex use the following operators:

x the character "x"

"x" an "x", even if x is an operator.

\x an "x", even if x is an operator.

[xy] the character x or y.

[x-z] the characters x, y or z.

[^x] any character but x.

. any character but newline.

^x an x at the beginning of a line.

<y>x an x when Lex is in start condition y.

x$ an x at the end of a line.

x? an optional x.

x* 0,1,2, ... instances of x.

x+ 1,2,3, ... instances of x.

x|y an x or a y.

(x) an x.

x/y an x but only if followed by y.

{xx} the translation of xx from the definitions section.

x{m,n} m through n occurrences of x

Lex Actions

When an expression written as above is matched, Lex executes the corresponding action. This section describes some features of Lex which aid in writing actions. Note that there is a default action, which consists of copying the input to the output. This is performed on all strings not otherwise matched. Thus the Lex user who wishes to absorb the entire input, without producing any output, must provide rules to match everything. When Lex is being used with Yacc, this is the normal situation. One may consider that actions are what is done instead of copying the input to the output; thus, in general, a rule which merely copies can be omitted. Also, a character combination which is omitted from the rules and which appears as input is likely to be printed on the output, thus calling attention to the gap in the rules.

One of the simplest things that can be done is to ignore the input. Specifying a C null statement, *;* as an action causes this result. A frequent rule is [\t\n] ; which causes the three spacing characters (blank, tab, and new line) to be ignored. In more complex actions, the user will often want to know the actual text that matched some expression like *[a-z]+*. Lex leaves this text in an external character array named *yytext.* Thus, to print the name found, a rule like [a-z]+ printf("%s", yytext); will print the string in *yytext.* The C function *printf* accepts a format argument and data to be printed; in this case, the format is "print string"

Sometimes it is more convenient to know the end of what has been found; hence Lex also provides a count *yyleng* of the number of characters matched. To count both the number of words and the number of characters in words in the input, the user might write [a-zA-Z]+ {words++; chars += yyleng;} which accumulates in *chars* the number of characters in the words recognized. The last character in the string matched can be accessed by yytext[yyleng-1]. In addition to these routines, Lex also permits access to the I/O routines it uses. They are:

1. *input()* which returns the next input character;
2. *output(c)* which writes the character *c* on the output; and
3. *unput(c)* pushes the character *c* back on to the input stream to be read later by *input().*

By default these routines are provided as macro definitions, but the user can override them and supply private versions. These routines define the relationship between external files and internal characters, and must all be retained or modified consistently. They may be redefined, to cause input or output to be transmitted to or from strange places, including other programs or internal memory; but the character set used must be consistent in all routines; a value of zero returned by *input* must mean end of file; and the relationship between *unput* and *input* must be retained or the Lex lookahead will not work. Lex does not look ahead at all if it does not have to, but every rule ending in + * *?* or *$* or containing */* implies lookahead. Lookahead is also necessary to match an expression that is a prefix of another expression.

Another Lex library routine that the user will sometimes want to redefine is *yywrap()* which is called whenever Lex reaches an end-of file. If *yywrap* returns a 1, Lex continues with the normal wrapup on end of input. Sometimes, however, it is convenient to arrange for more input to arrive from a new source. In this case, the user should provide a *yywrap* which arranges for new input and returns 0. This instructs Lex to continue processing. The default *yywrap* always returns 1.

This routine is also a convenient place to print tables, summaries, etc. at the end of a program. Note that it is not possible to write a normal rule which recognizes end-of-file; the only access to this condition is through *yywrap.* In fact, unless a private version of *input()* is supplied a file containing nulls cannot be handled, since a value of 0 returned by *input* is taken to be end-of-file.

Ambiguous Source Rules

Lex can handle ambiguous specifications. When more than one expression can match the current input, Lex chooses as follows:

1. The longest match is preferred.
2. Among rules which matched the same number of characters, the rule given first is preferred.

Usage

There are two steps in compiling a Lex source program. First, the Lex source must be turned into a generated program in the host general purpose language. Then this program must be compiled and loaded, usually with a library of Lex subroutines. The generated program is on a file named *lex.yy.c*. The I/O library is defined in terms of the C standard library.

The C programs generated by Lex are slightly different on OS/370, because the OS compiler is less powerful than the UNIX or GCOS compilers, and does less at compile time. C programs generated on GCOS and UNIX are the same. The library is accessed by the loader flag *-ll.* So an appropriate set of commands is

lex source cc lex.yy.c -ll

The resulting program is placed on the usual file *a.out* for later execution. (To use Lex with Yacc see below). Although the default Lex I/O routines use the C standard library, the Lex automata themselves do not do so; if private versions of *input, output* and *unput* are given, the library can be avoided.

9.2 Examples

(a) This program converts upper case to lower, removes blanks at the end of lines, and replaces multiple blanks by single blanks.

```
%%
[A–Z]        putchar(yytext[0]+'a'–'A');
```

```
[]+$
[]+          putchar(‘’);
```

(b) As a trivial problem, consider copying an input file while adding 3 to every positive number divisible by 7. Here is a suitable Lex source program

```
%%
        int k;
[0-9]+  {
        k = atoi(yytext);
        if (k%7 == 0)
           printf("%d", k+3);
        else
           printf("%d",k);
        }
```

to do just that. The rule [0-9]+ recognizes strings of digits; atoi converts the digits to binary and stores the result in k. The operator % (remainder) is used to check whether k is divisible by 7; if it is, it is incremented by 3 and it is written out.

9.2(a) Program & Logic

Implement the lexical analyzer using lex or other lexical analyzer generating tools

Input

```
main()
{
   int a,b;
   if ( a > b )
      printf(“hai”);
   else
      b=100; /* this is comment */
   }
```

Logic

- Define regular expressions for all tokens-keywords, ids, operators’ constants and comments.
- when input matches that pattern, define the action to be performed against each regular expression
- Include main() that calls yylex() function created by lex tool.
- Include yywrap() function which deal with EOF.

9.2(b) Lex Program

```
%{
#include<stdio.h>
int lineno=1;
%}
letter [a-zA-Z]
digit [0-9]
id {letter}({letter}|{digit})*
num {digit}+
kw "int"|"char"|"float"|"print"|"main"|"if"|"elseif"|"then"
arr ({id}"["({num}|{id})"]")
comm ("/*"({id}|"\n")*"*/")
ws [.,;'"]
%%                  /* Pattern matchning rules */
[\n]                {lineno++;}
{ws}                {printf("special sym=%s lineno=%d\n",yytext,lineno);}
">"|"<"|"<="|">="   {printf("rela ope=%s lineno=%d\n",yytext,lineno);}
{comm}              {printf("comment=%s lineno=%d\n",yytext,lineno);}
"="                 {printf("assignment oper=%s lineno=%d\n",yytext,lineno);}
"+"|"-"|"*"|"/"     {printf("operator=%s lineno=%d\n",yytext,lineno);}
"["|"]"|"{"|"}"|"("|")" {printf("paranthesys=%s lineno=%d\n",yytext,lineno);}
{kw}                {printf("keyword=%s lineno=%d\n",yytext,lineno);}
{arr}               {printf("array=%s lineno=%d\n",yytext,lineno);}
{id}                {printf("identifier=%s lineno=%d\n",yytext,lineno);}
{num}               {printf("number=%s lineno=%d\n",yytext,lineno);}
%%                  /* subroutines */
main(int argc,char **argv)
{
if(argc > 1)
yyin=fopen(argv[1],"r");
else
yyin= stdin;
yylex();
}
yywrap()
{
exit(0);
}
```

9.2(c) Results

Lexeme	Token	Line no
main	keyword	1
(	parenthesis	1
)	parenthesis	1
{	parenthesis	2
int	keyword	3
a	identifier	3
,	specialsym	3
b	identifier	3
;	senttermi	3
if	keyword	4
(	parenthesis	4
a	identifier	4
>	operator	4
b	identifier	4
)	parenthesis	4
printf	keyword	5
(	parenthesis	5
“	specialsym	5
hai	identifier	5
”	specialsym	5
)	parenthesis	5
;	senttermi	5
else	keyword	6
b	identifier	7
=	operator	7
100	keyconst	7
;	senttermi	7
/* this is comment */	comment	7
}	parenthesis	8

9.3 Viva Questions

1. What is LEX?

   lex is a tool for generating scanners: programs which recognizes lexical patterns in source text

2. What are three different sections of LEX program?

    Definitions

    Translation rules

    Subroutines

3. Explain the purpose of each section of LEX program?

    Definitions section contains names for regular expressions

    Translation rules section contains regular expressions and actions against it.

    Subroutines part contains supporting functions.

4. Write the general form of translation rule section of LEX program?

    Regular Expressions {actions}

5. What is the output of Lex compiler?

    yylex program in lex.yy.c file.

6. What are the routines compulsory in subroutine section?

    main(), yywrap()

7. Give lex program to delete all blanks or tabs at the ends of lines.

```
%%
   [ \t]+$  ;
```

8. Give lex program to count number of lines in text.

```
%{
        int lno;
}%
%%
   [\n]       {lno++;}
```

9. What is default 'c' file name Lex produces after compiling Lex program to c program?

    lex.yy.c

10. What is advantage of using Lex tool over hand written Lexical analyzer module?

    Lex automatically converts regular expressions to table driven automata and uses that automata in recognizing tokens.

9.4 Exercises

Divide the following statements to tokens using Lex tool.

1. for (i=0 , j=0 ; i<10 ; i++ j++)
2. int x,y,z,a,b,c;
3. while(i<10) i=i+10;

CHAPTER 10

Recursive Descent Parser

10.1 Introduction

One of the most straightforward forms of parsing is recursive descent parsing. This is a top-down process in which the parser attempts to verify that the syntax of the input stream is correct as it is read from left to right. A basic operation necessary for this involves reading characters from the input stream and matching them with terminals from the grammar that describes the syntax of the input. Our recursive descent parsers will look ahead one character and advance the input stream reading pointer when proper matche occurs. The routine presented in Fig. 10.1 accomplishes this matching and reading process

Recursive descent parser actually performs a depth-first search of the derivation tree for the string being parsed. This provides the 'descent' portion of the name. The 'recursive' portion comes from the parser's form, a collection of recursive procedures.

10.2 Example

As our first example, consider the simple grammar

$$\mathbf{E} \rightarrow \mathrm{x+T}$$
$$\mathbf{T} \rightarrow \mathrm{(E)}$$
$$\mathbf{T} \rightarrow \mathrm{x}$$

and the derivation tree for the expression x+(x+x)

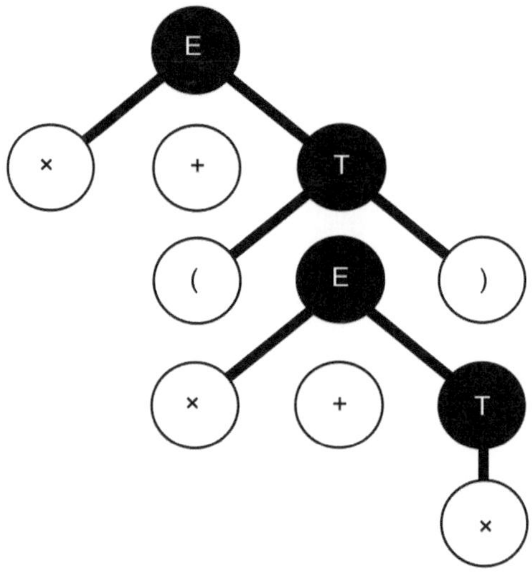

Fig 10.1 Derivation Tree for x+(x+x).

10.2(a) Program & Logic

A recursive descent parser traverses the tree by first calling a procedure to recognize an E. This procedure reads an 'x' and a '+' and then calls a procedure to recognize a T.

Let next_token be the next token in the input stream. match() is the action of recognizing the next token in the parsing process and advancing the input stream pointer, such that next_token points to the next token to be parsed. match() is effectively a call to the lexical analyzer to get the next token. This would look like the following routine.

```
char next;

next=getchar();

int match(char token)

      { if next==token then next=getchar();

        else errorhandler();

      }
```

Note that 'errorhandler' is a procedure that notifies the user that a syntax error has been made and then possibly terminates execution.

E → x+T

for this rule procedure for E is defined as follows.

```
Procedure E( )
  {  if next=='x' {
                    match('x');
                    match('+');
                     T( );
                    }
              else errorhandler();
  }
```

T → (E)
T → x

In order to recognize a T, the parser must figure out which of the productions to execute. This is not difficult and is done in the procedure that appears below.

```
Procedure T( )
{  if next=='(' {
                    match('(');
                    E( );
                    match(')');
                     T( );
                    }
     {  if next=='x' {
                    match('x');
                          }
              else errorhandler();
}
```

In the above routine, the parser determines whether T had the form (E) or x. If not then the error routine was called, otherwise the appropriate terminals and nonterminals were recognized.

So, one needs to write a recursive descent parser is a nice grammar which is free of left recursion and is left factored.

10.2(b) Coding

Design Recursive descent parser for the following Grammar

Input

$E \rightarrow T E'$

$E' \rightarrow +TE' \mid \varepsilon$

$T \rightarrow FT'$

$T' \rightarrow *FT' \mid \varepsilon$

$F \rightarrow i$

```
/* Recursive descent parser in C*/
#include <stdio.h>
#include <conio.h>
void E();
void E' ();
void T();
void T' ();
void F();
void match(char);
 int flag=1;
char l,t;`

main()
{
Printf("enter input string\n");
scanf("%c",&l);
E();
}

/*Procedure for matching terminal with token */
void match(char t)
{
```

```
if(l==t)
scanf("%c",&l);
 else
{
 flag=0;
         }
    }

/*Procedure for nonterminal E */

void E()
  {
    T();
    E' ();
    if((l=='$')&&(flag !=0) )
printf("successful\n");
else
printf("unsuccessful\n");
}

/*Procedure for nonterminal E´ */

void E' ()
{
    if(l=='+')
    {match('+');
    T();
    E' ();
    }
    else return;
}

/*Procedure for nonterminal T */

void T()
{
    F();
    T' ();
}
```

```
/*Procedure for nonterminal T′ */

void T′ ()
{
if(l=='*')
    {match('*');
    F();
    T' ();
    }
    else return;
}

/*Procedure for nonterminal F */

void F()
{
    match('i');
}
```

10.2(c) Results

Enter the input string:

```
i+i*i$
successful
i**i$
unsuccessful.
```

10.3 Viva Questions

1. What is recursive descent parser?

   Recursive descent parser is a top-down parser which verifies the syntax of the input stream as it is read from left to right.

2. Is left factoring is compulsory in designing recursive descent parser?

   No

3. Is left recursion is compulsory in designing recursive descent parser?

   Yes

4. What are the advantages of recursive descent parser?

   Simple to construct.

5. What are the disadvantages of recursive descent parser?

   Can be designed for small languages
   They cannot parse in pot that require arbitrarily long lookaheads

6. How do you design a recursive descent parser?

   By writing recursive procedures for every nonterminal.

7. How do you decide the number of procedures to be defined?

   Generally depends on number of nonterminals. For every nonterminal there should be a procedure.

8. Can the procedure be recursive?

   Yes. It depends on the production that is defined for the nonterminal. If production is recursive then procedure also will be recursive.

9. Can you use this technique for any language?

   No. Not suitable for left recursive grammers.

10. Can we design a recursive descent parser with ambiguous grammar

    No

10.4 Exercise Problems

Construct a recursive descent parser to parse the string 'w' for the given grammar 'G'

1. w = id*id + id & grammar is $E \to E + T \mid T \quad T \to T * F \mid F \quad F \to id \mid (E)$
2. w = id + id*id & grammar is $E \to E + T \mid T \quad T \to T\ F \mid F \quad F \to F * \mid a \mid b$
3. w = bdc & grammar is $S \to Aa \mid bAc \mid dc \mid bda \quad A \to d$

   type → simple
   type → ↑ id
   type → array [simple] of type
   simple → integer
   simple → char
   simple → num dotdot num

w = array [num dotdot num] of integer

CHAPTER 11

Predictive Parser-LL(1) Parser

11.1 Introduction

It is possible to build a LL(1) parser by maintaining a stack explicitly, rather than implicitly via recursive calls. The key problem during predictive parsing is that of determining the production to be applied for a nonterminal. The Nonrecursive parser looks up the production to be applied in parsing table. We shall see how the table can be constructed directly from certain grammars.

A table-driven predictive parser has an input buffer, a stack, a parsing table, and an output stream. The input buffer contains the string to be parsed, followed by $, a symbol used as a right end marker to indicate the end of the input string. The stack contains a sequence of grammar symbols with $ on the bottom, indicating the bottom of the stack. Initially, the stack contains the start symbol of the grammar on top of **$.** The parsing table is a two dimensional array M[A,a] where **A** is a nonterminal, and a is a terminal or the symbol **$.** The parser is controlled by a program that behaves as follows. The program considers **X,** the symbol on the top of the stack, and **a,** the current input symbol. These two symbols determine the action of the parser.

There are three possibilities.

1. If X= a=$, the parser halts and announces successful completion of parsing.
2. If X=a!=$, the parser pops X off the stack and advances the input pointer to the next input symbol.
3. If X is a nonterminal, the program consults entry M[X,a] of the parsing table M. This entry will be either an X-production of the grammar or an error entry. If, for example, M[X,a]={X→UVW}, the parser replaces X on top of the stack by WVU (with U on top). As output, we shall assume that the parser just prints the production used; any other code could be executed here. If M[X,a]=error, the parser calls an error recovery routine.

The behavior of the parser can be described in terms of its configurations, which give the stack contents and the remaining input.

Algorithm for LL(1) Parsing

Input: A string w and a parsing table M for grammar G.

Output: If w is in L(G), a leftmost derivation of w; otherwise, an error indication.

Method: Initially, the parser is in a configuration in which it has $S on the stack with S, the start symbol of G on top, and w$ in the input buffer. The program that utilizes the predictive parsing table M to produce a parse for the input.

```
set ip to point to the first symbol of w$.
repeat
    let X be the top stack symbol and a the symbol pointed to by ip.
    if X is a terminal of $ then
        if X=a then
            pop X from the stack and advance ip
        else error()
    else
        if M[X,a]=X→Y1Y2...Yk then begin
        pop X from the stack;
        push Yk,Yk-1...Y1 onto the stack, with Y1 on top;
        output the production X→ Y1Y2...Yk
    end
        else error()
until X=$
```

FIRST and FOLLOW

The construction of a predictive parser is aided by two functions associated with a grammar G. These functions, FIRST and FOLLOW, allow us to fill in the entries of a predictive parsing table for G, whenever possible. Sets of tokens yielded by the FOLLOW function can also be used as synchronizing tokens during panic-mode error recovery.

If x is any string of grammar symbols, let FIRST(x) be the set of terminals that begin the strings derived from x. If $x \overset{*}{\Rightarrow} \varepsilon$, then ε is also in FIRST(x).

Define FOLLOW(A), for nonterminals **A**, to be the set of terminals **a** that can appear immediately to the right of **A** in some sentential form, that is, the set of terminals **a** such that there exists a derivation of the form $S \overset{*}{\Rightarrow} xAab$ for some x and b. Note that there may, at some time during the derivation, have been symbold beteween A and a, but if so, they derived e and disappeared. If A can be the rightmost symbol in some sentential form, then $ is in FOLLOW(A).

To compute FIRST(X) for all grammar symbols X, apply the following rules until no more terminals or ε can be added to any FIRST set.

1. If X is terminal, then FIRST(X) is {X}.

2. If X→ε is a production, then add ε to FIRST(X).
3. If X is a nonterminal and X→Y1Y2...Yk is a production, then place 'a' in FIRST(X) if for some i, 'a' is in FIRST(Yi) and ε is in all of FIRST(Y1),...,FIRST(Yi-1); that is, Y1...Yi-1 $\overset{*}{\Rightarrow}$ ε. If ε is in FIRST(Yj) for all j=1,2,...,k, then add ε to FIRST(X). For example, everything in FIRST(Yj) is surely in FIRST(X). If y1 does not derive ε, then we add nothing more to FIRST(X), but if Y1 $\overset{*}{\Rightarrow}$ ε, then we add FIRST(Y2) and so on.

   Now, we can compute FIRST for any string X1X2X3...Xn as follows. Add to FIRST(X1X2X3...Xn) all the non-ε symbols of FIRST(X1). Also add the non-ε symbols of FIRST(X2) if ε is in FIRST(X1), the non-ε symbols of FIRST(X3) if ε is in both FIRST(X1) and FIRST(X2), and so on. Finally, add ε to FIRST(X1X2...Xn) if, for all i, FIRST(Xi) contains ε.

To compute the FOLLOW(A) for all nonterminals A, apply the following rules until nothing can be added to any FOLLOW set.

1. Place $ in FOLLOW(S), where S is the start symbol and $ in the input right end marker.
2. If there is a production A=>aBβ where FIRST(β) except ε is placed in FOLLOW(B).
3. If there is production A->aB or a production A->aBβ where FIRST(ß) contains ε, then everything in FOLLOW(A) is in FOLLOW(B).

Consider the following example to understand the concept of First and Follow

Find the first and follow of all nonterminals in the Grammar-

E → TE'
E'→ +TE'|ε
T → FT'
T'→ *FT'|ε
F → (E)|id

First(E) = {(, id}
First(E') = {+, ε}
First(T) = {(, id}
First(T') = {*, ε}
First(F) = {(, id}

Follow(E) = {$} by rule 1
= {)} by rule 2 on production F-> (E) | id
= {$,)}

Follow(E') = Follow(E) by rule 3 on production E -> T E'
= {$,)}

Follow(T) = First(E') by rule 2
= {+, ε}
= Follow(E) by rule 3 on production E -> T E'
= {$,)}
= {+,), $}

Follow(T') = Follow(T) by rule 3 on production T -> F T'
= {+,), $}

Follow(F) = First(T') by rule 2
= {*}
= Follow(T) by rule 3 on production T -> F T'
= {+,), $}
= Follow(T') by rule 3 on production T' -> F T'
= {+,), $}
= {+,), *, $}

FOLLOW(E)=FOLLOW(E')={),$}
FOLLOW(T)=FOLLOW(T')={+,),$}
FOLLOW(F)={+,*,),$}

For example, id and left parenthesis are added to FIRST(F) by rule 3 in definition of FIRST with i=1 in each case, since FIRST(id)=(id) and FIRST('(')= {(} by rule 1. Then by rule 3 with i=1, the production T -> FT' implies that id and left parenthesis belong to FIRST(T) also.

To compute FOLLOW, we put $ in FOLLOW(E) by rule 1 for FOLLOW. By rule 2 applied to production F→ (E), right parenthesis is also in FOLLOW(E). By rule 3 applied to production E → TE', $ and right parenthesis are in FOLLOW(E').

Construction of LL(1) Table

For any grammar G, the following algorithm can be used to construct the predictive parsing table. The algorithm is:

Input : Grammar G

Output : Parsing table M

Method

1. For each production A → a of the grammar, do steps 2 and 3.
2. For each terminal a in FIRST(a), add A → a, to M[A,a].
3. If ε is in First(a), add A → a to M[A,b] for each terminal b in FOLLOW(A). If ε is in FIRST(a) and $ is in FOLLOW(A), add A → a to M[A,$].
4. Make each undefined entry of M as error.

LL(1) Grammar

The above algorithm can be applied to any grammar G to produce a parsing table M. For some Grammars, for example if G is left recursive or ambiguous, then M will have at least one multiply-defined entry.

A grammar whose parsing table has no multiply defined entries is said to be LL(1). It can be shown that the above algorithm can be used to produce for every LL(1) grammar G a parsing table M that parses all and only the sentences of G. LL(1) grammars have several distinctive properties. No ambiguous or left recursive grammar can be LL(1). There remains a question of what should be done in case of multiply defined entries. One easy solution is to eliminate all left recursion and left factoring, hoping to produce a grammar which will produce no multiply defined entries in the parse tables. Unfortunately there are some grammars which will not give an LL(1) grammar after any kind of alteration. In general, there are no universal rule to convert multiply defined entries into single valued entries without affecting the language recognized by the parser.

The main difficulty in using predictive parsing is in writing a grammar for the source language such that a predictive parser can be constructed from the grammar. Although left recursion elimination and left factoring are easy to do, they make the resulting grammar hard to read and difficult to use for translation. To alleviate some of this difficulty, a common organization for a parser in a compiler is to use a predictive parser for control constructs and to use operator precedence for expressions. However, if an LR parser generator is available, one can get all the benefits of predictive parsing and operator precedence automatically.

Error Recovery in Predictive Parsing

The stack of a Nonrecursive predictive parser makes explicit the terminals and nonterminals that the parser hopes to match with the remainder of the input. We shall therefore refer to symbols on the parser stack in the following discussion. An error is detected during predictive parsing when the terminal on top of the stack does not match the next input symbol or when nonterminal **A** is on top of the stack, **a** is the next input symbol, and the parsing table entry M[A,a] is empty.

Panic-mode error recovery is based on the idea of skipping symbols on the input until a token in a selected set of synchronizing tokens appears. Its effectiveness depends on the choice of synchronizing set. The sets should be chosen so that the parser recovers quickly from errors that are likely to occur in practice. Some heuristics are as follows:

1. As a starting point, we can place all symbols in FOLLOW(A) into the synchronizing set for nonterminal A. If we skip tokens until an element of FOLLOW(A) is seen and pop A from the stack, it is likely that parsing can continue.
2. It is not enough to use FOLLOW(A) as the synchronizing set for A. For example, if semicolons terminate statements, as in C, then keywords that begin statements may not appear in the FOLLOW set of the nonterminal generating expressions. A missing semicolon after an assignment may therefore result in the keyword beginning the next statement being skipped. Often, there is a hierarchical structure on constructs in a language; e.g., expressions appear within statement, which appear within blocks, and so on. We can add to the synchronizing set of a lower construct the symbols that begin higher constructs. For example, we might add keywords that begin statements to the synchronizing sets for the nonterminals generating expressions.
3. If we add symbols in FIRST(A) to the synchronizing set for nonterminal A, then it may be possible to resume parsing according to A if a symbol in FIRST(A) appears in the input.
4. If a nonterminal can generate the empty string, then the production deriving ε can be used as a default. Doing so may postpone some error detection, but cannot cause an error to be missed. This approach reduces the number of nonterminals that have to be considered during error recovery.
5. If a terminal on top of the stack cannot be matched, a simple idea is to pop the terminal, issue a message saying that the terminal was inserted, and continue parsing. In effect, this approach takes the synchronizing set of a token to consist of all other tokens.

11.2 Example

E → TE'

E'→ +TE'|ε

T → FT'

T'→ *FT'|ε

F → (E)|id

LL(1) Table for the above grammar is

Nonterminal	(	id	+	*	)	$
E	T E'	T E'				
E'			+T E'		ε	ε
T	F T'	F T'				
T'			ε	*F T'	ε	ε
F	(E)	id				

11.2(a) Program & Logic

Design Predictive parser/LL(1) parser

Program Logic

- **Input is LL(1) table and input string to be parsed.**
- **Read terminals in array 't'. This is used as columns of table.**
- **Read nonterminals in array 'nt' This is used as rows of table.**
- **Now read table in two dimensional array of strings 'table'.**
- **Fist inialize the stack with $ and start symbol.**
- **Use parsing algorithm to parse input string.**
- **Whenever top of the stack is a nonterminal, to replace that by corresponding production- use two functions getnt() , gett() to get row and column in table.**
- **Take the production from that row & column, reverse it and push symbol by symbol.**
- **Continue till top of the stack is $ and input pointer points to $, the right end marker.**

11.2(b) Coding

```
/* LL(1) parser in C      */
#include<stdio.h>
#include<ctype.h>
#include<string.h>
char table[10][10][10], nt[10],t[10],inp[20],stack[20];
int nut,nun,i=0,top=0;
int getnt(char);
int gett(char);
void replace(char,char);
```

```
int main()
{
int i,j;
      /* read terminals and nonterminals   */
printf("Enter number of terminals\n");
scanf("%d",&nut);
printf("Enter number of nonterminals\n");
scanf("%d",&nun);
printf("Enter all non terminals\n");
scanf("%s",nt);
printf("Enter all terminals\n");
scanf("%s",t);

printf("\n");
printf("\n");
      /* Read Table*/
for(i=0;i<nun;i++)
for(j=0; j<nut;j++)
 {
   printf("Enter for %c and %c        ",nt[i],t[j]);
    scanf("%s",table[i][j]);
  }

      /* Print Table*/
 printf("Table is \n\n");
 for(j=0;j<nut;j++)
   printf("\t %c",t[j]);
 printf("\n");
 for(i=0;i<nun;i++)
 {
 printf("%c \t",nt[i]);
 for(j=0;j<nut;j++)
   {
    printf("%s \t",table[i][j]);
  }
  printf("\n");
 }
      /* Read input string to be parsed*/
```

```
printf("Enter the string to parse\n");
scanf("%s",inp);

    /* LL(1) parsing algorithm begins*/

stack[top++]='$';
stack[top++]=nt[0];
i=0;
while(1)
{
  if((stack[top-1]=='$')&&(inp[i]=='$'))
  {
    printf("String accepted\n");
    return;
  }
  else if(!isupper(stack[top-1]))
  {
    if(stack[top-1]==inp[i])
    {
       i++; top--;
    }
    else
    {
       printf("error not accepted\n");
       return;
    }
  }
  else
  {
    replace(stack[top-1],inp[i]);
  }
}

}

      /* get index of nonterminals in nonterminals array */

int getnt(char x)
{
```

```
 int a;
 for(a=0;a<nun;a++)
  if(x==nt[a]) return a;
 return 100;
}
```

/* get index of terminals in terminals array */

```
int gett(char x)
{
 int a;
 for(a=0;a<nut;a++)
  if(x==t[a]) return a;
 return 100;
}
void replace(char NT, char T)
{
 int in1,it1,len;
 char str[10];
 in1=getnt(NT);
 it1=gett(T);
 if((in1!=100)&&(it1!=100))
 {
  strcpy(str,table[in1][it1]);
  if(strcmp(str,"#")==0)
  {
   printf("Error\n");
   return ;
  }
  if(strcmp(str,"@")==0)
   top--;
  else
  {
   top--;
   len=strlen(str);
   len--;
   do
   {
```

```
      stack[top++]=str[len--];
    }while(len>=0);
   }
  }
  else
  {
   printf("Not valid\n");
  }
 }
```

11.2(C) Results

```
$ ./a.out

Enter number of terminals
6
Enter number of nonterminals
5
Enter all non terminals
EATBF
Enter all terminals
i+*()$

Enter for E and i      TA
Enter for E and +      #
Enter for E and *      #
Enter for E and (      TA
Enter for E and )      #
Enter for E and $      #
Enter for A and i      #
Enter for A and +      +TA
Enter for A and *      #
Enter for A and (      #
Enter for A and )      @
Enter for A and $      @
Enter for T and i      FB
Enter for T and +      #
Enter for T and *      #
Enter for T and (      FB
```

```
Enter for T and )     #
Enter for T and $     #
Enter for B and i     #
Enter for B and +     @
Enter for B and *     *FB
Enter for B and (     #
Enter for B and )     @
Enter for B and $     @
Enter for F and i     i
Enter for F and +     #
Enter for F and *     #
Enter for F and (     (E)
Enter for F and )     #
Enter for F and $     #
```

Table is

	i	+	*	(	)	$
E	TA	#	#	TA	#	#
A	#	+TA	#	#	@	@
T	FB	#	#	FB	#	#
B	#	@	*FB	#	@	@
F	i	#	#	(E)	#	#

```
Enter the string to parse
i+i*i$

String accepted
```

11.3 Viva Questions

1. What is meant by LL(1) ?
   - First L indicates scanning of input from left to right
   - Second L indicates that parser uses LMD in deriving the string
   - "1" indicates number of look ahead symbols used in taking the parsing decisions.
2. What are the requirements for LL(1) parser?
   - Grammar should be free of left recusrsion and should be left factored.

3. Is LL(1) parser a top down parser or bottom up parser.
    - Top down parser
4. Can every unambiguous grammer be parsed by LL(1)
    - No
5. What is the advantage of eliminating left recursion
    - Avoids parser going into infinite loop.
6. What is the advantage of left factoring
    - Avoids backtracking.
7. What is an ambiguous grammar
    - A grammar which has more than one parse tree using either LMD or RMD for a string is called ambiguous grammar
8. How to eliminate left recursion for $A \rightarrow A\ \alpha \mid \beta$
    - $A \rightarrow \beta\ A'$
    - $A' \rightarrow \alpha\ A' \mid \varepsilon$
9. How to eliminate left factor the grammar $A \rightarrow \alpha\ \beta_1 \mid \alpha\ \beta_2 \mid \alpha\ \beta_3$
    - $A \rightarrow \alpha\ A'$
    - $A' \rightarrow \beta_1 \mid \beta_2 \mid \beta_3$
10. Is every LL(1) unambiguous?
    - yes

11.4 Exercise Problems

Construct an LL(1) parser to parse the string 'w' for the given grammar 'G'

1. w=id*id+id & grammar is $E \rightarrow E + T \mid T \quad T \rightarrow T * F \mid F \quad F \rightarrow id \mid (E)$
2. w= id+ id*id & grammar is $E \rightarrow E + T \mid T \quad T \rightarrow T\ F \mid F \quad F \rightarrow F * \mid a \mid b$
3. w=111000 & grammar is $S \rightarrow 1S0 \mid 0S1 \mid 10$

CHAPTER 12

LALR Parser

12.1 Introduction

It is a bottom up parser which is a compromise between SLR(1) and LR(1). LALR(1) Stands for Look-Ahead LR

- A LALR(1) parser for G has
  - The same number of states as an SLR parser.
  - Some of the lookahead discrimination of LR(1).
- LALR languages are not natural.
  - They are an efficiency hack on LR languages
- Any reasonable programming language has an LALR(1) grammar.
- LALR(1) has become a standard for programming languages and for parser generators.

Because a canonical LR(1) parser splits states based on differing lookahead sets, it can have many more states than the corresponding SLR(1) or LR(0) parser. Potentially it could require splitting a state with just one item into a different state for each subset of the possible lookaheads; in a pathological case, this means the entire power set of its follow set (which theoretically could contain all terminals). A canonical LR(1) parser for a programming language might have more states than an SLR(1) parser. With LALR (*lookahead LR*) parsing, we attempt to reduce the number of states in an LR(1) parser by merging similar states. This reduces the number of states to the same as SLR(1), but still retains some of the power of the LR(1) lookaheads.

Let's examine the LR(1) configurating sets from an example given Grammar G1 in the LR parsing .

```
        S' -> S
        S -> XX
        X -> aX
        X -> b
I0:     S' -> •S, $
```

```
      S -> •XX, $
      X -> •aX, a/b
      X -> •b, a/b
I1:   S' -> S•, $
I2:   S -> X•X, $
      X -> •aX, $
      X -> •b, $
I3:   X -> a•X, a/b
      X -> •aX, a/b
      X -> •b, a/b
I4:   X -> b•, a/b
I5:   S -> XX•, $
I6:   X -> a•X, $
      X -> •aX, $
      X -> •b, $
I7:   X -> b•, $
I8:   X -> aX•, a/b
I9:   X -> aX•, $
```

Notice that some of the LR(1) states look suspiciously similar. Take I_3 and I_6 for example. These two states are virtually identical—they have the same number of items, the core of each item is identical, and they differ only in their lookahead sets. This observation may make you wonder if it possible to merge them into one state. The same is true of I_4 and I_7, and I_8 and I_9. If we did merge, we would end up replacing those six states with just these three:

```
I36:    X -> a•X, a/b/$
        X -> •aX, a/b/$
        X -> •b, a/b/$
I47:    X -> b•, a/b/$
I89:    X -> aX•, a/b/$
```

But isn't this just SLR(1) all over again? In the above example, yes, since after the merging we coincidentally end up with the complete follow sets as the lookahead. This is not always the case however. Consider this example Grammar G2.

```
S' -> S
S -> Bbb | aab | bBa
B -> a
I0:  S' -> •S, $
```

```
     S -> •Bbb, $
     S -> •aab, $
     S -> •bBa, $
     B -> •a, b
I1:  S' -> S•, $
I2:  S -> B•bb, $
I3:  S -> a•ab, $
     B -> a•, b
     ....
```

In an SLR(1) parser there is a shift-reduce conflict in state 3 when the next input is anything in Follow(B)which includes a and b. In LALR(1), state 3 will shift on ‘a’ and reduce on ‘b’. Intuitively, this is because the LALR(1) state "remembers" that we arrived at state 3 after seeing an ‘a’. Thus we are trying to parse either Bbb or aab. In order for that first ‘a’ to be a valid reduction to B, the next input has to be exactly ‘b’ since that is the only symbol that can follow B in this particular context. Although elsewhere an expansion of B can be followed by an ‘a’, we consider only the subset of the follow set that can appear here, and thus avoid the conflict an SLR(1) parser would have.

LALR Merge Conflicts

Can merging states in this way ever introduce new conflicts? A shift-reduce conflict cannot exist in a merged set unless the conflict was already present in one of the original LR(1) configurating sets. When merging, the two sets must have the same core items. If the merged set has a configuration that shifts on ‘a’ and another that reduces on a, both configurations must have been present in the original sets, and at least one of those sets had a conflict already. Reduce-reduce conflicts, however, are another story. Consider the following grammar:

```
S' -> S
S -> aBc | bCc | aCd | bBd
B -> e
C -> e
```

The LR(1) configurating sets are as follows:

```
I0:  S' -> •S, $
     S -> •aBc, $
     S -> •bCc, $
     S -> •aCd, $
     S -> •bBd, $
I1:  S' -> S•, $
```

```
I2:  S -> a•Bc, $
     S -> a•Cd, $
     B -> •e, c
     C -> •e, d
I3:  S -> b•Cc, $
     S -> b•Bd, $
     C -> •e, c
     B -> •e, d
I4:  S -> aB•c, $
I5:  S -> aC•d, $
I6:  B -> e•, c
     C -> e•, d
I7:  S -> bC•c, $
I8:  S -> bB•d, $
I9:  B -> e•, d
     C -> e•, c
I10: S -> aBc•, $
I11: S -> aCd•, $
I12: S -> bCc•, $
I13: S -> bBd•, $
```

We try to merge I_6 and I_9 since they have the same core items and they only differ in lookahead:

```
I69: C -> e, c/d
B -> e, d/c
```

However, this creates a problem. The merged configurating set allows a reduction to either B or C when next token is c or d. This is a reduce-reduce conflict and can be an unintended consequence of merging LR(1) states. When such a conflict arises in doing a merging, we say the grammar is not LALR(1).

LALR Table Construction

A LALR(1) parsing table is built from the configurating sets in the same way as canonical LR(1); the lookaheads determine where to place reduce actions. In fact, if there are no mergable states in the configuring sets, the LALR(1) table will be identical to the corresponding LR(1) table and we gain nothing.

In the common case, however, there will be states that can be merged and the LALR table will have fewer rows than LR. The LR table for a typical programming language may have several thousand rows, which can be merged into just a few hundred for LALR. Due to merging, the LALR(1) table seems more similar to the SLR(1) and LR(0) tables, all three have the same number of states (rows), but the LALR may have fewer reduce actions—some reductions are not valid if we are more precise about the lookahead. Thus, some conflicts are avoided because an action cell with conflicting actions in SLR(1) or LR(0) table may have a unique entry in an LALR(1) once some erroneous reduce actions have been eliminated.

LALR(1) Table Construction

There are two ways to construct LALR(1) parsing tables. The first (and certainly more obvious way) is to construct the LR(1) table and merge the sets manually. This is sometimes referred as the "brute force" way. If you don't mind first finding all the multitude of states required by the canonical parser, compressing the LR table into the LALR version is straightforward.

1. Construct all canonical LR(1) states.
2. Merge those states that are identical if the lookaheads are ignored, i.e., two states being merged must have the same number of items and the items have the same core (i.e., the same productions, differing only in lookahead). The lookahead on merged items is the union of the lookahead from the states being merged.
3. The successor function for the new LALR(1) state is the union of the successors of the merged states. If the two configurations have the same core, then the original successors must have the same core as well, and thus the new state has the same successors.
4. The action and goto entries are constructed from the LALR(1) states as for the canonical LR(1) parser. Consider the LR(1) table for the grammar G1 given. There are nine states.

State on top of stack	Action			Goto	
	a	b	c	S	X
0	s3	s4		1	2
1			Acc		
2	s6	s7			5
3	s3	s4			8
4	r3	r3			
5			r1		
6	s6	s7			9
7			r3		
8	r2	r2			
9			r2		

Looking at the configurating sets, we saw that states 3 and 6 can be merged, so can 4 and 7, and 8 and 9. Now we build this LALR(1) table with the six remaining states:

State on top of stack	Action			Goto	
	a	b	$	S	X
0	s36	s47		1	2
1			Acc		
2	S36	S47			5
36	S36	s47			89
47	r3	r3	r3		
5			r1		
89	r2	r2	r2		9

The More Clever Approach

Having to compute the LR(1) configurating sets first means we won't save any time or effort in building an LALR parser. However, the work wasn't all for naught, because when the parser is executing, it can work with the compressed table, thereby saving memory. The difference can be an order of magnitude in the number of states.

However there is a more efficient strategy for building the LALR(1) states called *step-bystep merging*. The idea is that you merge the configurating sets as you go, rather than waiting until the end to find the identical ones. Sets of states are constructed as in the LR(1) method, but at each point where a new set is spawned, you first check to see whether it may be merged with an existing set. This means examining the other states to see if one with the same core already exists. If so, you merge the new set with the existing one, otherwise you add it normally.

LALR(1) Grammars

A formal definition of what makes a grammar LALR(1) cannot be easily encapsulated in a set of rules, because it needs to look beyond the particulars of a production in isolation to consider the other situations where the production appears on the top of the stack and what happens when we merge those situations. Instead we state that what makes a grammar LALR(1) is the absence of conflicts in its parser. If you build the parser and it is conflict-free, it implies the grammar is LALR(1) and vice-versa.

LALR(1) is a subset of LR(1) and a superset of SLR(1). A grammar that is not LR(1) is definitely not LALR(1), since whatever conflict occurred in the original LR(1) parser will still be present in the LALR(1). A grammar that is LR(1) may or may not be LALR(1) depending on whether merging introduces conflicts. A grammar that is SLR(1) is definitely LALR(1). A grammar that is not SLR(1) may or may not be LALR(1) depending on whether the more precise lookaheads resolve the SLR(1) conflicts.

LALR(1) has proven to be the most used variant of the LR family. The weakness of the SLR(1) and LR(0) parsers mean they are only capable of handling a small set of grammars. The expansive memory needs of LR(1) caused it to languish for several years as a theoretically interesting but intractable approach. It was the advent of LALR(1) that offered a good balance between the power of the specific lookaheads and table size. The popular tools **yacc** and **bison** generate LALR(1) parsers and most programming language constructs can be described with an LALR(1) grammar

Handling Errors

The LALR parser may continue to do reductions after the LR parser would have spotted an error, but the LALR parser will never do a shift after the point the LR parser would have discovered the error and will eventually find the error.

LR Parsing Algorithm

Input : Input string *w* and an LR parsing table with functions action and goto for a grammar *G*.

Output: If *w* is in L(*G*), it halts in accepting state. Otherwise, an error indication is given.

Method: Initially the parser has s_0, the initial state, on its stack, and *w*$ in the input buffer.

```
repeat forever begin
        let ‘s’ be the state on top of the stack
            and ‘a’ the symbol pointed to by ip;
        if action[s, a] = shift s' then begin
            push a, then push s' on top of the stack;  // <symbol, state> pair
            advance ip to the next input symbol;
        else if action[s, a] = reduce A -> β then begin
            pop 2* |β| symbols off the stack;
            let s' be the state now on top of the stack;
            push A, then push goto[s', A] on top of the stack;
            output the production A -> β; // for example
        else if action[s, a] = accept then
            return
        else error();
end
```

12.2 Example

Construct LR(1) and LALR(1) parsing tables for the following grammar.

S → CC

C → cC

C → d

Sets of LR(1) items

I_0: S'->.S,$

S->.CC,$

C->.Cc,c/d

C->.d,c/d

I_1: S'->S.,$

I_2: S->C.C,$

C->.Cc,$

C->.d,$

I_3: C->c.C,c/d

C->.Cc,c/d

C->.d,c/d

I_4: C->d.,c/d

I_5: S->CC.,$

I_6: C->c.C,$

C->.cC,$

C->.d,$

I_7: C->d.,$

I_8: C->cC.,c/d

I_9: C->cC.,$

LR(1) Parsing Table is:

	action			Go to	
State	**C**	**d**	**$**	**S**	**C**
0	S3	S4		1	2
1			acc		
2	S6	S7			5
3	S3	S4			8
4	R3	R3			
5			R1		
6	S6	S7			9
7			R3		
8	R2	R2			
9			R2		

DFA is

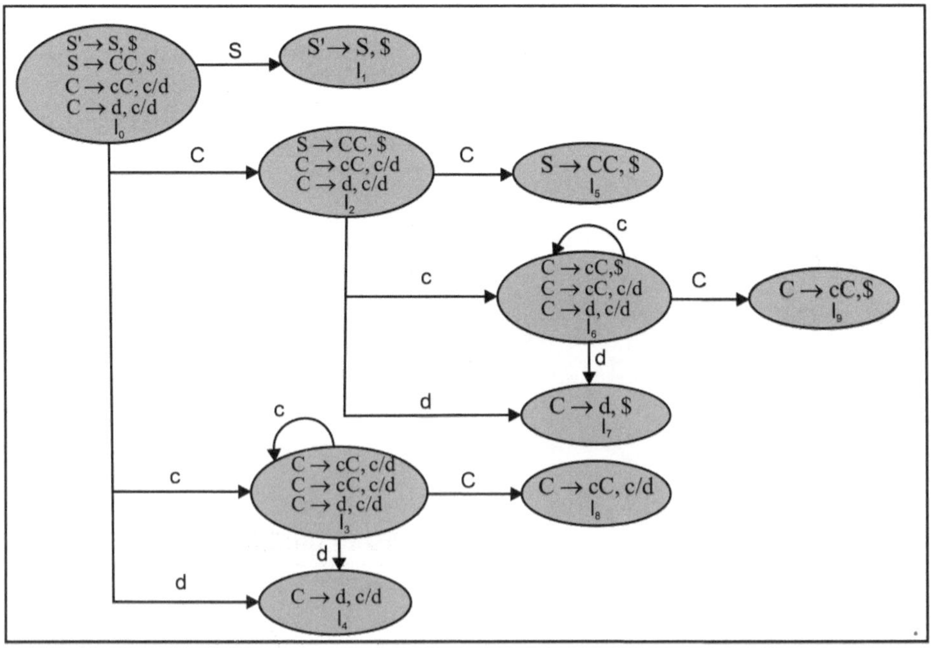

LALR(1) Parsing Table

- If two (or more) states in an LR(1) PDA are identical except for look ahead, then the states can be merged
- This leads to a compressed table

Consider the above example,

I_3 & I_6 can be replaced by their union

I_{36}: C->c.C,c/d/$

C->.Cc,C/D/$

C->.d,c/d/$

I_{47}: C->d.,c/d/$

I_{89}: C->Cc.,c/d/$

	action			go to	
state	c	d	$	S	C
0	s36	s47		1	2
1			acc		
2	s36	s47			5
36	s36	s47			89
47	r3	r3	r3		
5			r1		
89	r2	r2	r2		

For a given grammar, no.of states of SLR(1) and LALR(1) is always equal.

12.2(a) Program and Logic

Input for the parser is LR table & string to be parsed.

Read terminals and nonterminals.This is used as columns of the table.

Read states. This is used as rows of the table.

- **Now read action part in 'action' table and goto part in 'goto' table.**
- **Fist inialize the stack with $ and state 0.**
- **Use LR parsing algorithm**
- **When top of the stack is state 1 & input is $, halt.**

12.2(b) Coding

```
/* Design LR parser. */
#include<stdio.h>
#include<ctype.h>
#include<string.h>
#include<stdlib.h>
char action[20][10][2], nt[10],t[10],inp[20],stack[20][2],a[3];
char pro[20][10],str[10],str2[10],state[20][2],gto[20][10][2];
int t1,s1,x;
int nut,nun,i=0,top=0,np,numst,nent,k;
int getnt(char);
int gett(char);
int getst(char *);
void main()
{
int i,j,len,n1,n2,i1,j1;
char ch,ans='y',temp[5];
clrscr();
/* read terminals , nonterminals,productions   & Table*/
printf("Enter number of terminals\n");
scanf("%d",&nut);
printf("Enter number of non terminals\n");
scanf("%d",&nun);
printf("Enter number of productions\n");
scanf("%d",&np);
for(i=0;i<np;i++)
{
 printf("Enter production\n");
scanf("%s",pro[i]);
}
```

```
for(i=0;i<np;i++)
{
printf("production %s\n",pro[i]);
}
printf("Enter all non terminals\n");
scanf("%s",nt);
printf("Enter all terminals\n");
scanf("%s",t);
for(i=0;i<nut;i++) printf("%c\t",nt[i]);
printf("\n");
for(j=0;j<nun;j++) printf("%c\t",t[j]);
printf("\n");
printf("Enter number of states\n");
scanf("%d",&numst);
for(i=0;i<numst;i++)
{
printf("Enter state name\n");
scanf("%s",state[i]);
}
printf("Enter action as s2 for shift 2\n r2 for reduce 2\nac for accept\ne for
error\n");
for(i=0;i<numst;i++)
for(j=0; j<nut;j++)
{
strcpy(action[i][j],"");
printf("Enter for %d and %c",i,t[j]);
scanf("%s",action[i][j]);
}
for(j=0;j<nut;j++)
printf("\t %c",t[j]);
printf("\n");
```

```
for(i=0;i<numst;i++)
{
printf("%c \t",nt[i]);
for(j=0;j<nut;j++)
{
printf("%s \t",action[i][j]);
}
printf("\n");
}
for(i=0;i<numst;i++)
for(j=0;j<nun;j++)
{
strcpy(gto[i][j],"");
}
printf("Enter number of entries\n");
scanf("%d",&nent);
for( k=0;k<nent;k++)
{
printf("Enter state number");
scanf("%d",&i1);
flushall();
printf("Enter Non terminal");
scanf("%c",&ch);
j1=getnt(ch);
flushall();
printf("enter goto[%d][%d]\n",i1,j1);
scanf("%c",gto[i1][j1]);
}
do
{
strcpy(inp,"");
```

```
/* read input string to be parsed */

printf("Enter the string to parse\n");
scanf("%s",inp);

/* LR parsing begins */

top=0;
strcpy(stack[top++],"$");
strcpy(stack[top++],"0");
i=0;
while(1)
{
t1=gett(inp[i]);
s1=getst(stack[top-1]);
strcpy(str,action[s1][t1]);
if(str[0]=='a')
{
printf("String accepted\n");
break;
}
else if(str[0]=='s')
{
temp[0]=inp[i++];
temp[1]='\0';
strcpy(stack[top++],temp);
for(i1=0;i1<strlen(str);i1++)
if((i1!=0) && isdigit(str[i1])) temp[i1-1]=str[i1];
strcpy(stack[top++],temp);
}
else if(str[0]=='r')
{
a[0]=str[1];
```

```
a[1]='\0';
x=atoi(a);
strcpy(str2,pro[x]);
len=strlen(str2);
len=len-3;
top=top-2*len;
temp[0]=str2[0];
temp[1]='\0';
strcpy(stack[top++],temp);
n1=getst(stack[top-2]);
n2=getnt(str2[0]);
strcpy(stack[top++],gto[n1][n2]);
}
else
{
printf("Error not valid string\n");
break;
}
}
flushall();
ch=' ';
printf("Do you want to continue\n");
scanf("%c",&ch);
}while(ans=='y');
}
int getnt(char x)
{
int a;
for(a=0;a<nun;a++)
i f(x==nt[a]) return a;
return 100;
```

```
}
int gett(char x)
{
int a;
for(a=0;a<nut;a++)
if(x==t[a]) return a;
return 100;
}
int getst(char st[])
{
int l;
for(l=0;l<numst;l++)
if(strcmp(st,state[l])==0) return l;
return 100;
}
```

12.2(c) Results

```
Enter number of terminals
3
Enter number of non terminals
2
Enter number of productions
4
Enter production
A->S
Enter production
S->CC
Enter production
C->cC
Enter production
C->d
Production
A->S
```

```
S->CC
C->Cc
C->d
Enter all non terminals
SC
Enter all terminals
cd$
Enter number of states
10
Enter state name 0
Enter state name 1
Enter state name 2
Enter state name 3
Enter state name 4
Enter state name 5
Enter state name 6
Enter state name 7
Enter state name 8
Enter state name 9
Enter action as s2 for shift 2
r2 for reduce 2
ac for accept
e for error
Enter for 0 and c s3
Enter for 0 and d s4
Enter for 0 and $ e
Enter for 1 and c e
Enter for 1 and d e
Enter for 1 and $ ac
Enter for 2 and c s6
Enter for 2 and d s7
Enter for 2 and $ e
Enter for 3 and c s3
Enter for 3 and d s4
```

Enter for 3 and $ e
Enter for 4 and c e
Enter for 4 and d e
Enter for 4 and $ r
Enter for 5 and c s3
Enter for 5 and d s4
Enter for 5 and $ e
Enter for 6 and c s3
Enter for 6 and d s4
Enter for 6 and $ e
Enter for 7 and c s3
Enter for 7 and d s4
Enter for 7 and $ e
Enter for 8 and c s3
Enter for 8 and d s4
Enter for 8 and $ e
Enter for 9 and c s3
Enter for 9 and d s4
Enter for 9 and $ e
Enter number of entries
5
Enter state number 0
Enter Non terminal S
enter goto[0][0]
1
Enter state number 0
Enter Non terminal C
enter goto[0][1]
2
Enter state number 2
Enter Non terminal C
enter goto[2][2]
5
Enter state number 3

```
Enter Non terminal C
enter goto[3][1]
8
Enter state number 6
Enter Non terminal C
enter goto[6][1]
9
Enter the string to parse
dd$
String accepted
Do you want to continue
y
Enter the string to parse
cdcd$
String accepted
Do you want to continue
n
```

12.3 Viva Questions

1. What is meant by LALR parser
    - Look ahead LR parser
2. What is the other name of LR parser
    - SR parser or bottom up parser
3. What are the advantages of bottom up parsers?
    - They are powerful
    - No restrictions on grammars to construct bottom up parsers.
4. Can you design a LR parser for left recursive grammar
    - Yes
5. Compare LALR(1) with LR(1)?
    - LR(1) is the most powerful parser but requires more table space than LALR(1). Hence LALR(1) is widely used .Yacc uses LALR(1) tecqnique.
6. Compare LALR(1) with SLR(1)
    - SLR(1) is less powerful than LALR(1).

7. Compare table sizes of LALR(1) and SLR(1)
   - Same size
8. For a given grammar, if SLR(1) has n1 states, LALR(1) has n2 states and LR(1) has n3 states, what is the relation on states?
   - (n1== n2) <= n3
9. How the number of states in LALR(1) are reduced?
   - LALR(1) reduces the number of states by merging states with similar items but differing by lookahead.
10. Which type of items are used by LR(1) ?
    - LR(1) items

12.4 Exercises

Construct LALR parser for the following grammars

1. $S \rightarrow + S S \mid * S S \mid a$
2. $S \rightarrow AaAb \mid BbBa$

   $A \rightarrow \varepsilon$

   $B \rightarrow \varepsilon$
3. $S \rightarrow Aa \mid bAc \mid dc \mid bda$

   $A \rightarrow d$

   4. $S \rightarrow Aa \mid bAc \mid Bc \mid bBa$

   $A \rightarrow d$

   $B \rightarrow d$

CHAPTER 13

Yacc-Yet Another Compiler

13.1 Introduction

Yacc provides a general tool for imposing structure on the input to a computer program. The Yacc user prepares a specification of the input process. This includes rules describing the input structure, code to be invoked when these rules are recognized, and a low-level routine to do the basic input. Yacc then generates a function to control the input process. This function, called a *parser*, calls the user-supplied low level input routine (the *lexical analyzer*) to pick up the basic items (called *tokens*) from the input stream.

These tokens are organized according to the input structure rules, called *grammar rules*. When one of these rules has been recognized, then user code supplied for this rule, an *action*, is invoked; actions have the ability to return values and make use of the values of other actions. Yacc is written in a portable dialect of C and the actions, and output subroutine, are in C as well. Moreover, many of the syntactic conventions of Yacc follow C. The heart of the input specification is a collection of grammar rules. Each rule describes an allowable structure and gives it a name.

For example, one grammar rule might be

```
date : month day ',' year ;
```

Here, *date*, *month*, *day*, and *year* represent structures of interest in the input process; presumably, *month*, *day*, and *year* are defined elsewhere. The comma ``,'' is enclosed in single quotes; this implies that the comma is to appear literally in the input. The colon and semicolon merely serve as punctuation in the rule, and have no significance in controlling the input. Thus, with proper definitions, the input July 4, 1776 might be matched by the above rule.

Every specification file consists of three sections: the *declarations*, *(grammar) rules*, and *programs*. The sections are separated by double percent ``%%'' marks. (The percent ``%'' is generally used in Yacc specifications as an escape character.)

In other words, a full specification file looks like

```
declarations
%%
rules
```

```
%%
programs
```

The declaration section may be empty. Moreover, if the programs section is omitted, the second %% mark may be omitted also; thus, the smallest legal Yacc specification is

```
%%
rules
```

With each grammar rule, the user may associate actions to be performed each time the rule is recognized in the input process. These actions may return values, and may obtain the values returned by previous actions. Moreover, the lexical analyzer can return values for tokens, if desired.

An action is an arbitrary C statement, and as such can do input and output, call subprograms, and alter external vectors and variables.

To return a value, the action normally sets the pseudo-variable ''$$'' to some value. For example, an action that does nothing but return the value 1 is { $$ = 1; }

To obtain the values returned by previous actions and the lexical analyzer, the action may use the pseudo-variables $1, $2, . . ., which refer to the values returned by the components of the right side of a rule, reading from left to right. Thus, if the rule is A : B C D ;

then $2 has the value returned by C, and $3 the value returned by D.

As a more concrete example, consider the rule

```
expr : '(' expr ')' ;
```

The value returned by this rule is usually the value of the *expr* in parentheses. This can be indicated by

```
expr : '(' expr ')' { $$ = $2 ; }
```

Lexical Analysis

The user must supply a lexical analyzer to read the input stream and communicate tokens (with values, if desired) to the parser. The lexical analyzer is an integer-valued function called *yylex*. The function returns an integer, the *token number*, representing the kind of token read. If there is a value associated with that token, it should be assigned to the external variable *yylval*. The parser and the lexical analyzer must agree on these token numbers in order for communication between them to take place. The numbers may be chosen by Yacc, or chosen by the user. In either case, the ''# define'' mechanism of C is used to allow the lexical analyzer to return these numbers symbolically.

For example, suppose that the token name DIGIT has been defined in the declarations section of the Yacc specification file.

```
yylex(){
extern int yylval;
int c;
. . .
c = getchar();
. . .
switch( c ) {
. . .
case '0':
case '1':
. . .
case '9':
yylval = c-'0';
return( DIGIT );
. . .
}
. . .
```

The intent is to return a token number of DIGIT, and a value equal to the numerical value of the digit. Provided that the lexical analyzer code is placed in the programs section of the specification file, the identifier DIGIT will be defined as the token number associated with the token DIGIT.

The machine has only four actions available to it, called *shift*, *reduce*, *accept*, and *error*. A move of the parser is done as follows:

1. Based on its current state, the parser decides whether it needs a lookahead token to decide what action should be done; if it needs one, and does not have one, it calls *yylex* to obtain the next token.
2. Using the current state, and the lookahead token if needed, the parser decides on its next action, and carries it out. This may result in states being pushed onto the stack, or popped off of the stack, and in the lookahead token being processed or left alone.

The *shift* action is the most common action the parser takes. Whenever a shift action is taken, there is always a lookahead token.

The *reduce* action keeps the stack from growing without bounds. Reduce actions are appropriate when the parser has seen the right hand side of a grammar rule, and is prepared to announce that it has seen an instance of the rule, replacing the right hand side by the left hand side. It may be necessary to consult the lookahead token to decide whether to reduce, but usually it is not; in fact, the default action (represented by a ".") is often a reduce action. Suppose the rule being reduced is

```
A : x y z ;
```

The reduce action depends on the left hand symbol (A in this case), and the number of symbols on the right hand side (three in this case). To reduce, first pop off the top three states from the stack. In effect, these states were the ones put on the stack while recognizing *x* , *y* , and *z* , and no longer serve any useful purpose. After popping these states, a state is uncovered which was the state the parser was in before beginning to process the rule. Using this uncovered state, and the symbol on the left side of the rule, perform what is in effect a shift of A. A new state is obtained, pushed onto the stack, and parsing continues. There are significant differences between the processing of the left hand symbol and an ordinary shift of a token, however, so this action is called a *goto* action. In particular, the lookahead token is cleared by a shift, and is not affected by a goto.

The reduce action is also important in the treatment of user-supplied actions and values. When a rule is reduced, the code supplied with the rule is executed before the stack is adjusted. In addition to the stack holding the states, another stack, running in parallel with it, holds the values returned from the lexical analyzer and the actions. When a shift takes place, the external variable *yylval* is copied onto the value stack. After the return from the user code, the reduction is carried out. When the *goto* action is done, the external variable *yyval* is copied onto the value stack. The pseudo-variables $1, $2, etc., refer to the value stack.

The other two parser actions are conceptually much simpler. The *accept* action indicates that the entire input has been seen and that it matches the specification. This action appears only when the lookahead token is the endmarker, and indicates that the parser has successfully done its job.

The *error* action, on the other hand, represents a place where the parser can no longer continue parsing according to the specification.

Consider example! Consider the specification

```
%token DING DONG DELL
%%
rhyme : sound place
;
sound: DING DONG
;
place : DELL
;
```

When Yacc is invoked with the **-v** option, a file called *y.output* is produced, with a human-readable description of the parser.

Disambiguating Rules

Yacc invokes two disambiguating rules by default:

1. In a shift/reduce conflict, the default is to do the shift.
2. In a reduce/reduce conflict, the default is to reduce by the *earlier* grammar rule (in the input sequence).

The precedences and associativities are attached to tokens in the declarations section. This is done by a series of lines beginning with a Yacc keyword: %left, %right, or %nonassoc, followed by a list of tokens. All of the tokens on the same line are assumed to have the same precedence level and associativity;the lines are listed in order of increasing precedence or binding strength. Thus,

```
%left '+' '-'
%left '*' '/'
```

describes the precedence and associativity of the four arithmetic operators. Plus and minus are left associative, and have lower precedence than star and slash, which are also left associative. The keyword %right is used to describe right associative operators, and the keyword %nonassoc is used to describe operators, like the operator .LT. in Fortran, that may not associate with themselves; thus,

```
A .LT. B .LT. C
```

is illegal in Fortran, and such an operator would be described with the keyword %nonassoc in Yacc.

The Yacc Environment

When the user inputs a specification to Yacc, the output is a file of C programs, called *y.tab.c* on most systems (due to local file system conventions, the names may differ from installation to installation).The function produced by Yacc is called *yyparse*; it is an integer valued function. When it is called, it inturn repeatedly calls *yylex*, the lexical analyzer supplied by the user to obtain input tokens. Eventually, either an error is detected, in which case (if no error recovery is possible) *yyparse* returns the value 1, or the lexical analyzer returns the endmarker token and the parser accepts. In this case, *yyparse* returns the value 0. The user must provide a certain amount of environment for this parser in order to obtain a working program. For example, as with every C program, a program called *main* must be defined, that eventually calls *yyparse*. In addition, a routine called *yyerror* prints a message when a syntax error is detected. These two routines must be supplied in one form or another by the user. To ease the initial effort of using Yacc, a library has been provided with default versions of *main* and *yyerror*. The name of this library is system dependent;

on many systems the library is accessed by a **-ly** argument to the loader. To show the triviality of these default programs, the source is given below:

```
main(){
return( yyparse() );
}
```

and

```
# include <stdio.h>
yyerror(s) char *s; {
fprintf( stderr, "%s\n", s );
}
```

The argument to *yyerror* is a string containing an error message, usually the string ''syntax error''. The average application will want to do better than this. Ordinarily, the program should keep track of the input line number, and print it along with the message when a syntax error is detected. The external integer variable *yychar* contains the lookahead token number at the time the error was detected; this may be of some interest in giving better diagnostics. Since the *main* program is probably supplied by the user (to read arguments, etc.) the Yacc library is useful only in small projects, or in the earliest stages of larger ones. The external integer variable *yydebug* is normally set to 0. If it is set to a nonzero value, the parser will output a verbose description of its actions, including a discussion of which input symbols have been read, and what the parser actions are. Depending on the operating environment, it may be possible to set this variable by using a debugging system.

Preparing Specifications

This section contains miscellaneous hints on preparing efficient, easy to change, and clear specifications. The individual subsections are more or less independent.

Input Style

It is difficult to provide rules with substantial actions and still have a readable specification file. The following style hints owe much to Brian Kernighan.

(a) Use all capital letters for token names, all lower case letters for nonterminal names.

(b) Put grammar rules and actions on separate lines. This allows either to be changed without an automatic need to change the other.

(c) Put all rules with the same left hand side together. Put the left hand side in only once, and let all following rules begin with a vertical bar.

(d) Put a semicolon only after the last rule with a given left hand side, and put the semicolon on a separate line. This allows new rules to be easily added.

(e) Indent rule bodies by two tab stops, and action bodies by three tab stops.

Support for Arbitrary Value Types

By default, the values returned by actions and the lexical analyzer are integers. Yacc can also support values of other types, including structures. In addition, Yacc keeps track of the types, and inserts appropriate union member names so that the resulting parser will be strictly type checked. The Yacc value stack is declared to be a *union* of the various types of values desired. The user declares the union, and associates union member names to each token and nonterminal symbol having a value. When the value is referenced through a $$ or $n construction, Yacc will automatically insert the appropriate union name, so that no unwanted conversions will take place.

There are three mechanisms used to provide for this typing. First, there is a way of defining the union; this must be done by the user since other programs, notably the lexical analyzer, must know about the union member names. Second, there is a way of associating a union member name with tokens and nonterminals. Finally, there is a mechanism for describing the type of those few values where Yacc can not easily determine the type.

To declare the union, the user includes in the declaration section:

```
%union {
body of union ...
}
```

This declares the Yacc value stack, and the external variables *yylval* and *yyval* , to have type equal to this union. If Yacc was invoked with the **-d** option, the union declaration is copied onto the *y.tab.h* file. Alternatively, the union may be declared in a header file, and a typedef used to define the variable YYSTYPE to represent this union. Thus, the header file might have:

```
typedef union {
body of union ...
} YYSTYPE;
```

The header file must be included in the declarations section, by use of %{ and %}.

Once YYSTYPE is defined, the union member names must be associated with the various terminal and nonterminal names. The construction

```
< name >
```

is used to indicate a union member name. If this follows one of the keywords %token, %left, %right, and

%nonassoc, the union member name is associated with the tokens listed. Thus, saying

```
%left <optype> '+' '-'
```

will cause any reference to values returned by these two tokens to be tagged with the union member name *optype*. Another keyword, %type, is used similarly to associate union member names with nonterminals. Thus, one might say

```
%type <nodetype> expr stat
```

13.2 Example

Consider the example of yacc program for evaluation of expressions.

yacc program

```
%{
#include<stdio.h>
%}
%token  NUM
%%
L:L E '\n'        {printf("value of expr=%d\n",$2);}
|;
E:E'+'T           {$$=$1+$3;}
| T
;
T:T'*' F          {$$=$1*$3;}
|F
;
F:NUM             {$$=$1;}
;
%%
main()
{
yyparse();
}
void yyerror(char *s)
{printf("error\n");
}
yylex()
{
```

```
char c;
while((c=getchar())!='\n')
{
if(isdigit(c))
{
yylval=c-'0';
return NUM;
}
else return c;
}
return c;
}
```

Output

```
$ yacc pl.y – μ
$ gcc y.tab.c.
$.\a.out
2 + 3 × 4
12
```

13.3 Generate Abstract Syntax Tree

BNF Rules for generating syntax tree.

Production	**Semantic Rule**
L → **L** E '\n'	Printtree(E.nptr);
E → E + T	E.nptr := mknode('+', E.nptr ,T.nptr)
| T	E.nptr :=T.nptr
T → T * F	T.nptr := mknode('* ', T.nptr ,F.nptr)
| F	T.nptr := F.nptr
F → **id**	F.nptr := mknode(**id.**place,NULL,NULL)

13.3(a) Program Logic

- **Input is a+b*c**
- Create lex.yy.c for tokens in input using lex tool.
- Write yacc program.
- To create tree, define a structure 'node' with three arguments – operator, left ptr, right ptr.
- yacc stack type default is integer which is defined in YYSTYPE. But now to store node pointers or ids, overwrite stack type by using %union with char type or node pointer type.
- Now to translate above SDT to yacc specification.

- Specify type of terminals by %token<type tag> nonterminals.
- Now $$ & $i refers to corresponding type of attribute.
- mknode() fuction is used to create a node with three arguments and returns pointer to newly created node.
- printtree() – function performs inorder traversal of tree and displays it.

13.3(b) Coding

LEX program

```
%%
[ \t]           {}
[a-zA-Z]*            {sscanf(yytext,"%c",&yylval);return id;}
[\n]           {return(yytext[0]);}
[+*-/]         {return(yytext[0]);}
%%
yywrap()
{
return 1;
}
```

Name this as tree.l and compile using lex compiler

tree.l→ [Lex] **→ lex.yy.c**

This is lexical analyzer in c.

Add it at supporting routines of yacc instead of writing yylex();

YACC – Program

```
        /*Declarations */
%{
#include<stdio.h>
#include<ctype.h>
typedef struct x
{
 char ch;
 struct x *lptr;
```

```
  struct x *rptr;
}node;
node *mknode(char ,node*,node*);
void printtree( node* );
%}
        /* Changing stack type      */
%union{
char idtype;
node *nptr;
}
%type <nptr> E T F L
%token<idtype> id
        /*Rules */
%%
L:L E '\n'        { printtree($2);}
|;
E:E '+' T         {$$=mknode('+',$1,$3);}
|T            {$$=$1;}
;
T:T '*' F         {$$=mknode('*',$1,$3);}
|F     {$$=$1;}
;
F:id          {$$=mknode($1,NULL,NULL);}
;
%%
#include "lex.yy.c"
main()
{  printf("The syntax tree  is\n");
yyparse();
}
void yyerror(char *s)
   {
   printf("error\n");
   }
```

```
    /* Creating nodes */
node *mknode(char c, node *lp, node *rp)
{
node *t;
t=(node *)malloc(sizeof(node));
t->ch=c;
t->lptr=lp;
t->rptr=rp;
return t;
}
    /* Traversing the tree */
void printtree (node *root)
{
if(root!=NULL)
{
    post(root->lptr);
    printf("%c\t",root->ch);
   post(root->rptr);
 }
}
```

Name this as tree.y and compile using yacc compiler

Compile y.tab.c using gcc

tree.y→ [Yacc] **→ y.tab.c**

y.tab.c→ [C compiler] **→ a.out**

13.3(c) Results

$lex tree.l

This gives output as lex.yy.c which is a lexer in c under a function name yylex().

$yacc tree.y

This gives output as y.tab.c which is a parser in c under a function name yyparse().

With –v option ($yacc –v tree.y), produces file y.output- which gives complete information about the LALR parser like DFA states, conflicts, no.of terminals used etc.

```
$cc y.tab.c
$./a.out
a+b*c
output:a+b*c.
```

13.4 Viva Questions

1. What is YACC?
    - Yet another compiler compiler. YACC is a parser generator.
2. What are three different sections in YACC program?
    - Declarations, translation rules and routines
3. What is the role of yylex() function in YACC program?
    - Whenever parser requires a token it automatically makes a call to yylex() to get the next token.
4. What is the output of yacc compiler?
    - yyparse() in file y.tab.c
5. YACC implements which type of parser?
    - LALR(1)
6. What is yyparse()?
    - Parser in c
7. How does YACC uses Lexical analyzer?
    - By calling yylex()
8. What is default c file name after compiling yacc program to c program?
    - y.tab.c
9. How does it handles errors?
    - By error productions
10. What is the routine yyerror()?
    - To print error diagnostics on error.

CHAPTER 14

Three Address Code Generation

14.1 Introduction

Three-address statements are a kind of assembly code. Statements can have symbolic labels and there are statements for flow of control. A symbolic label represents the index of a three-address statement in the array holding intermediate code. Actual indices can be substituted for the labels either by making a separate pass, or by using "back patching," .

Here are the common three-address statements used:

1. Assignment statements of the form x: = y op z, where op is a binary arithmetic or logical operation.
2. Assignment instructions of the form x:= op y, where op is a unary operation. Essential unary operations include unary minus, logical negation, shift operators, and conversion operators that, for example, convert a fixed-point number to a floating-point number.
3. Copy statements of the form x: = y where the value of y is assigned to x.
4. The unconditional jump goto L. The three-address statement with label L is the next to be executed.
5. Conditional jumps such as if x relop y goto L. This instruction applies a relational operator (<, =, >=, etc.) to x and y, and executes the statement with label L next if x stands in relation relop to y. If not, the three-address statement following if x relop y goto L is executed next, as in the usual sequence.
6. Param x and call p, n for procedure calls and return y, where y representing a returned value is optional. Their typical use is as the sequence of three-address statements

```
param x1
param x2
param xn
call p, n
```

   generated as part of a call of the procedure p(x1, x2,..., xn). The integer n indicating the number of actual parameters in "call p, n" is not redundant because calls can be nested.

7. Indexed assignments of the form x: = y[i] and x [i]: = y. The first of these sets x to the value in the location i memory units beyond location y. The statement x[i]:=y sets the contents of the location i units beyond x to the value of y. In both these instructions, x, y, and i refer to data objects.
8. Address and pointer assignments of the form x: = &y, x: = *y and *x: = y.

The first of these sets the value of x to be the location of y. Presumably y is a name, perhaps a temporary, that denotes an expression with an I-value such as A[i, j], and x is a pointer name or temporary. That is, the r-value of x is the l-value (location) of some object. In the statement x: = ~y, presumably y is a pointer or a temporary whose r- value is a location. The r-value of x is made equal to the contents of that location. Finally, + x: = y sets the r-value of the object pointed to by x to the r-value of y.

The choice of allowable operators is an important issue in the design of an intermediate form. The operator set must clearly be rich enough to implement the operations in the source language. A small operator set is easier to implement on a new target machine. However, a restricted instruction set may force the front end to generate long sequences of statements for some source, language operations. The optimizer and code generator may then have to work harder if good code is to be generated.

Syntax Directed Definition for Generating three address code:

S → id := E	{emit(P':=' E.place)}
E → E + T	{E.place := newtemp;
	emit(E.place ':='E.place '+' T.place)}
| T	{E.place=T.place}
T → T * F	{T.place ;= newtemp;
	emit(T.place ':=' T.place '*' F.place)}
| F	{T.place := F.place}
F → id	{ F.place:= id.name }

When three-address code is generated, temporary names are made up for the interior nodes of a syntax tree. The value of non-terminal E on the left side of E → E1 + T will be computed into a new temporary variable t. In general, the three- address code for id: = E consists of code to evaluate E into some temporary t, followed by the assignment id.place: = t. If an expression is a single identifier, say y, then y itself holds the value of the expression. The S-attributed definition generates three-address code for assignment statements. The non-terminal E has two attributes:

1. E.place, the name that will hold the value of E, and
2. E.code, the sequence of three-address statements evaluating E.

14.2 Example

Translate the following segment to three address code

```
for(i=0;i<=20;i++)
x=y+z;
```

```
100: i=1;
101: if (i<=20) goto 103
102: goto last
103: t=y+z
104:x=t
105: i=i+1
106 goto 101
last:
```

14.3 Generate Three Address Code

14.3(a) program Logic

- Write yylex() for recognizing tokens in input or use lex tool.
- Now to translate above SDD to yacc specification.
- Specify terminals by %token or by ' ' to recognize as it is.
- Remaining grammar symbols are treated as non terminals.
- $$ refers to attribute value associated with nonterminals on left hand side i.e. E.val.
- $i refers to attribute value associated with i^{th} grammar symbol on right hand side i.e. T.val.
- Use p,q as temporary variables in generating three address code.

14.3(b) Coding

lex program:

```
opr    [*+-/=]
%%
[ \t]          {}
[a-zA-Z]*        {sscanf(yytext,"%c",&yylval);return id;}
[\n]            {return(yytext[0]);}
```

```
{opr}      {return(yytext[0]);}
%%
yywrap()
{
return 1;
}
```

Yacc program

```
%{
#include<stdio.h>
#include<ctype.h>
int i=1;
%}
%token  id
%%
L:id'='E '\n'        {printf("%c=%c\n",$1,$3);}
   |;
E:E'+'T                        {$$='p';printf("%c=%c+%c\n",$$,$1,$3);}
    | T
    ;

T:T'*' F                       {$$='q';printf("%c=%c*%c\n",$$,$1,$3);}
  |F
    ;
F:id            {$$=$1;}
;
%%
#include "lex.yy.c"

main()
{printf("Three address code is\n");
yyparse();
}
void yyerror(char *s)
{printf("error\n");
}
```

```
/*int yylex()
{
char c;
while((c=getchar())!='\n')
{
if(isdigit(c))
{
yylval=c;
return id;
}
else return c;
}
return c;
}*/
```

14.3(c) Results

```
$ ./a.out
x=a+b*c
Three address code is
p=b*c
q=a+p
x=q
```

14.4 Viva Questions

1. What is the role of intermediate code generator in compilation process?
   - It prepares intermediate representation of source language which makes the target code generation easier.
2. What are different intermediate code representations?
   - Syntax tree, DAG, postfix notation, three address code.
3. Give different representations of three address code statement?
   - Quadruples, triples and indirect triples.
4. What is three address code statements?
   - Every statement contains maximum of three addresses in three address code.

5. What is polish notation?
   - Post fix representation of statement is polish notation.
6. What is the advantage of generating intermediate code?
   - It makes the target code generation easier.
7. What is DAG?
   - Directed acyclic graph
8. What is the advantage of DAG?
   - We can easily detect common subexpressions
9. Write three address code for -(a+b)+(c+d)+(a+b+c)?

   t1=a+b

   t2=-t1

   t3=c+d

   t4=t2+t3

   t5=a+b

   t6=t5+c

   t7=t4+t6
10. What is difference between tree and DAG?
    - Nodes for common subexpressions are created only once and reused in DAG

14.5 Exercise Problems

Generate three address code for following

1. while a<b do

   a=b+c;
2. while a<b do

   if c<d then x= y+z else x=y-z;
3. a<b and c<d
4. if (x<y) then x=100 else x=10;

CHAPTER 15

Target Code Generator

15.1 Introduction

The final phase in our compiler model is the **Target code generator**. It takes input in intermediate representation of the source program and produces output an equivalent target program.

The requirements traditionally imposed on a code generator are several. The output code must be correct and of high quality, meaning that it should make effective use of the resources of the target machine. Moreover, the code generator itself should run efficiently.

Issues in the Design of a Code Generator

While the details are dependent on the target language and the operating system, issues such as memory management, instruction selection, register allocation, and evaluation order are inherent in almost all code generation problems.

Input to the Code Generator

The input to the code generator consists of the intermediate representation of the source program produced by the front end, together with information in the symbol table that is used to determine the run time addresses of the data objects denoted by the names in the intermediate representation.

There are several choices for the intermediate language, including: linear representations such as postfix notation, three address representations such as quadruples, virtual machine representations such as syntax trees and dags.

We assume that prior to code generation the front end has scanned, parsed, and translated the source program into a reasonably detailed intermediate representation, so the values of names appearing in the intermediate language can be represented by quantities that the target machine can directly manipulate (bits, integers, reals, pointers, etc). We also assume that the necessary type checking has taken place, so type conversion operators have been inserted wherever necessary and obvious semantic errors (e.g., attempting to index an array by a floating point number) have already been detected. The code generation phase can therefore proceed on the assumption that its input is free of errors. In some compilers, this kind of semantic checking is done together with code generation.

Target Programs

The output of the code generator is the target program. The output may take on a variety of forms: absolute machine language, relocatable machine language, or assembly language.

Producing an absolute machine language program as output has the advantage that it can be placed in a fixed location in memory and immediately executed. A small program can be compiled and executed quickly. A number of "student-job" compilers, such as WATFIV and PL/C, produce absolute code.

Producing a relocatable machine language program as output allows subprograms to be compiled separately. A set of relocatable object modules can be linked together and loaded for execution by a linking loader. Although we must pay the added expense of linking and loading if we produce relocatable object modules, we gain a great deal of flexibility in being able to compile subroutines separately and to call other previously compiled programs from an object module. If the target machine does not handle relocation automatically, the compiler must provide explicit relocation information to the loader to link the separately compiled program segments.

Producing an assembly language program as output makes the process of code generation somewhat easier .We can generate symbolic instructions and use the macro facilities of the assembler to help generate code .The price paid is the assembly step after code generation.

Because producing assembly code does not duplicate the entire task of the assembler, this choice is another reasonable alternative, especially for a machine with a small memory, where a compiler must uses several passes.

Memory Management

Mapping names in the source program to addresses of data objects in run time memory is done cooperatively by the front end and the code generator. We assume that a name in a three-address statement refers to a symbol table entry for the name.

If machine code is being generated, labels in three address statements have to be converted to addresses of instructions. This process is analogous to the "back patching". Suppose that labels refer to quadruple numbers in a quadruple array. As we scan each quadruple in turn we can deduce the location of the first machine instruction generated for that quadruple, simply by maintaining a count of the number of words used for the instructions generated so far. This count can be kept in the quadruple array (in an extra field), so if a reference such as j: *goto i* is encountered, and i is less than j, the current quadruple number, we may simply generate a jump instruction with the target address equal to the machine location of the first instruction in the code for quadruple i. If, however, the jump is forward, so i exceeds j, we must store on a list for quadruple i the location of the first machine instruction generated for quadruple j. Then we process quadruple i, we fill in the proper machine location for all instructions that are forward jumps to i.

Instruction Selection

The nature of the instruction set of the target machine determines the difficulty of instruction selection. The uniformity and completeness of the instruction set are important factors. If the target machine does not support each data type in a uniform manner, then each exception to the general rule requires special handling.

Instruction speeds and machine idioms are other important factors. If we do not care about the efficiency of the target program, instruction selection is straightforward. For each type of three address statement we can design a code skeleton that outlines the target code to be generated for that construct.

For example, every three address statement of the form x := y + z, where x, y, and z are statically allocated, can be translated into the code sequence

```
MOV y, R0   /* load y into register R0  */
ADD z, R0   /* add z to R0 */
MOV R0, x   /* store R0 into x */
```

Unfortunately, this kind of statement-by-statement code generation often produces poor code. For example, the sequence of statements

```
a := b + c
d := a + e
```

would be translated into

```
MOV   b, R0
ADD   c, R0
MOV   R0, a
MOV   a, R0
ADD   e, R0
MOV   R0, d
```

Here the fourth statement is redundant, and so is the third if 'a' is not subsequently used.

The quality of the generated code is determined by its speed and size.

A target machine with a rich instruction set may provide several ways of implementing a given operation. Since the cost differences between different implementations may be significant, a naive translation of the intermediate code may lead to correct, but unacceptably inefficient target code. For example if the target machine has an "increment" instruction (INC), then the three address statement a: = a+1 may be implemented more efficiently by the single instruction INC a, rather than by a more obvious sequence that loads a into a register, add one to the register, and then stores the result back into a.

```
MOV  a, R0
ADD  #1,R0
MOV  R0, a
```

Instruction speeds are needed to design good code sequence but unfortunately, accurate timing information is often difficult to obtain. Deciding which machine code sequence is best for a given three address construct may also require knowledge about the context in which that construct appears.

Register Allocation

Instructions involving register operands are usually shorter and faster than those involving operands in memory. Therefore, efficient utilization of register is particularly important in generating good code. The use of registers is often subdivided into two subproblems:

1. During **register allocation,** we select the set of variables that will reside in registers at a point in the program.
2. During a subsequent **register assignment** phase, we pick the specific register that a variable will reside in.

Finding an optimal assignment of registers to variables is difficult, even with single register values. Mathematically, the problem is NP-complete

Choice of Evaluation Order

The order in which computations are performed can affect the efficiency of the target code. Some computation orders require fewer registers to hold intermediate results than others. Picking a best order is another difficult, NP-complete problem. Initially, we shall avoid the problem by generating code for the three address statements in the order in which they have been produced by the intermediate code generator.

Approches to Code Generation

The most important criterion for a code generator is to produce correct code. Correctness takes on special significance because of the number of special cases that code generator must face. Given the premium on correctness, designing a code generator can be easily implemented, tested, and maintained.

A Simple Target Machine Model

The following is a simple register-based machine, supporting a total of 17 instructions, it has three distinct internal storage areas. The first is the set of 8 registers, used by the individual instructions as detailed below, the second is an area used for the storage of variables and the third is an area used for the storage of program. The instructions can be preceded by a label. This consists of an integer in the range 1 to 9999 and the label is followed by a colon to separate it from the rest of the instruction. The numerical label can be used as the argument to a jump instruction, as detailed below. In the description of the individual instructions below, instruction argument types are specified as follows:

R

specifies a register in the form RO, R1, R2, R3, R4, R5, R6 or R7 (or r0, r1, etc.).

L

specifies a numerical label (in the range 1 to 9999).

V

specifies a "variable location" (a variable number, or a variable location pointed to by a register – see below).

A

specifies a constant value, a variable location, a register or a variable location pointed to by a regi[ster] (an indirect address). Constant values are specified as an integer value, optionally preceded by[a] minus sign, preceded by a # symbol. An indirect address is specified by *an* @ followed by a register-So, for example, an A-type argument could have the form 4 (variable number 4), #4 (the constant valu[e] 4), r4 (register4) or @ r4 (the contents of register 4 identifies the variable location to be accessed).

The instruction set is defined as follows:

LOAD A,R

loads the integer value specified by A into register R.

STORE R,V

stores the value in register R to variable V.

OUT R

outputs the value in register R

NEG R

negates the value in register R.

ADD A,R

adds the value specified by A to register R, leaving the result in register R.

SUB A,R

subtracts the value specified by A from register R, leaving the result in register R.

MUL A,R

multiplies the value specified by A by register R, leaving the result in register R.

DIV A,R

divides register R by the value specified by A, leaving the result in register R.

JMPL

causes an unconditional jump to the instruction with the label L

JEQ R,L

jumps to the instruction with the label L if the value in register R is zero.

JNE R,L

jumps to the instruction with the label L if the value in register R is not zero.

JGE R,L

jumps to the instruction with the label L if the value in register R is greater than or equal to zero.

JGT R,L

jumps to the instruction with the label L if the value in register R is greater than zero.

JLE R,L

jumps to the instruction with the label L if the value in register R is less than or equal to zero.

JLT R,L

jumps to the instruction with the label L if the value in register R is less than zero.

NOP

is an instruction with no effect. It can be tagged by a label.

STOP

stops execution of the machine. All programs should terminate by executing a STOP instruction.

15.2 Example

Now consider the two three address code sequences (a) and (b) in which the only difference is the operator in the second statement. The shortest assembly sequence for (a) and (b) are given in(c).

Ri stands for register i. L, ST and A stand for load, store and add respectively. The optimal choice for the register into which ‘a’ is to be loaded depends on what will ultimately happen to e.

(a)	(b)
t := a + b	t := a + b
t := t * c	t := t + c
t := t / d	t := t / d

Fig 15.1 (a) & (b) three address code sequences.

(a)		(b)	
L	R1, a	L	R0, a
A	R1, b	A	R0, b
M	R0, c	A	R0, c
D	R0, d	SRDA	R0, 32
ST	R1, t	D	R0, d
		ST	R1, t

Fig. 15.2 Optimal machine code sequence for Fig. 15.1.

Program & Logic

- Take the input in post fix notation
- Use the logic of evaluation of postfix expression for generating target code.

Coding

Write program to generate machine code from the three address code generated by the parser.

```
PROGRAM:
#include<stdio.h>
#define max 20
static int r=0;
int top=-1;
char st[max];
void main()
 {
int h;
   char ip[10];
   clrscr();
```

```
printf("\n Enter the postfix expression:\n");
scanf("%s",ip);
h=0;
while(ip[h]!='\0')
{
while(islower(ip[h])!=0)
 {
   push(ip[h]);
   h++;
 }
getregister();
printf("load %c R%d\n",st[top-1],r);
switch(ip[h])
 {
   case '+':
    {
      printf("Add %c R%d \n",st[top],r);
      empty();
      h++;
    }
    break;
   case '*':
    {
      printf("Mul %c R%d \n",st[top],r);
      empty();
      h++;
    }
    break;
   case '-':
    {
      printf("Sub %c R%d \n",st[top],r);
      empty();
      h++;
    }
    break;
   case '/':
    {
```

```
                printf("Div  %c  R%d \n",st[top],r);
                empty();
                h++;
              }
              break;
             default:
               printf("\n Invalid case\n");
          }
      }
     getch();
  }
empty()
  {
     char t1;
     pop();
     pop();
     printf("str R%d t\n",r);
     t1='t';
     push(t1);
  }
getregister()
  {
      r++;
      if(r>2)
        r=1;
  }
push(char x)
  {
     if(top==max-1)
       printf("Stack is full\n");
     else
     {
      top++;
      st[top]=x;
     }
  }
```

```
pop()
 {
   if(top==-1)
      printf("Stack is empty\n");
   else
     top--;
 }
```

Result

```
 Enter the postfix expression:
abc*d/+e-
load  b  R1
Mul  c  R1
str R1 t
load  t  R2
Div  d  R2
str R2 t
load  a  R1
Add  t  R1
str R1 t
load  t  R2
Sub  e  R2
str R2 t
```